DEVOTIONS FOR TEENS

the LOOKING GLASS!

by Senior Staff
Camp Mini-Yo-We

EVERYDAY PUBLICATIONS INC.
230 Glebemount Avenue
Toronto, Canada M4C 3T4

ISBN   0-919586-30-9

Printed in Canada

THE LOOKING GLASS!

This is THE LOOKING GLASS #3. Each book gives you a few verses from the Bible for every day in the year. The whole series covers five years and goes through the Bible from Genesis to Revelation.

The writers are members of the senior staff of Camp Mini-Yo-We. These books will show you how the Bible speaks to the heart of anyone who will listen. They will also help you live for Christ every day.

THE LOOKING GLASS!

JANUARY 1   ACTS 7:1-10

This high priest was Caiaphas. He was the same one who was at Jesus' trial. Now he has Stephen before him talking again about this man Jesus. Stephen had spoken out against some Jewish teaching and was preaching the message of Jesus Christ.

In today's reading, Stephen is beginning a long talk about Jewish history. Later he will point out that Jesus is the Jews' promised Saviour.

How do you think Caiaphas felt? He thought he had finished with Jesus Christ. But here is Stephen speaking of Him in great power, claiming that He is still alive. God hadn't given up on Caiaphas. He was allowing him to hear of Jesus again. Will Caiaphas respond this time?

JANUARY 2   ACTS 7:11-21

The Jews had accused Stephen of speaking against Moses and God's law. They thought that it was very important to keep the commandments and the Jewish laws. In the next few verses Stephen shows that even though they had all these laws they still acted against God. Their laws kept them from obeying God rather than helped them obey Him.

Stephen wants them to realize that their Saviour, Jesus Christ, came to let them out of the prison of law keeping. He died so that they might be free. They just couldn't understand it.

Stephen talks about the beginning of Jewish history, Abraham and Moses. All this is leading up to the point Stephen wants to make. Jesus came to bring freedom.

5

JANUARY 3   ACTS 7:22-36

Moses thought of himself as a good man and a great leader who would free his people, the Israelites. He was ready to help them but had forgotten he had sinned against God. When he talked to the people about their wrongdoing they got very angry. Moses thought he was ready to help but God knew he was not. Moses had a lot to learn before God could really use him.

In many ways Moses was just like each of us. We think we are fairly good and know all we need to about God. But God knows this isn't true. He has much more to teach us. Are you trying to learn more about Him by reading your Bible, praying and going to church? Then maybe one day you will be ready for God to use you as He did Moses.

JANUARY 4   ACTS 7:37-50

Stephen has pointed out to the Jews that Moses wasn't as perfect as they thought. He was not trying to hurt their feelings but wanted them to understand that they needed Jesus Christ, not their prophets and laws.

In today's reading Stephen has another important idea to bring before the Jews. Their temple was very special to them and Stephen had been speaking against it. He tells them in verse 48 that God does not live in a building as they think. Although the Jews had built building after building for God they still didn't understand that He was too great for this. They had brought God to their level and were still ignoring Jesus Christ.

Is your God too small? Have you put Him in a box, or a church building or a 15-minute quiet time? Have you?

JANUARY 5   ACTS 7:51-60

How furious the Jews were with Stephen! He had spoken so strongly against them and their lack of understanding. He tells them (verse 51) that they had not listened to God's Holy Spirit. He speaks out against their relatives too.

Didn't Stephen know how angry this would make the people? Wasn't he scared to speak out so powerfully?

Yes, I'm sure he was scared. But his love and trust in Jesus Christ was stronger than his fear. He spoke out and was stoned to death.

You won't be killed if you speak out for Jesus Christ. But you might be laughed at. Can you take it? Stephen could and did. And Jesus took him to live with him for ever.

JANUARY 6   ACTS 8:1-8

Did you notice what Saul had done in Chapter 7? He really hated these Christians. He was a good Jew and loved God so he thought hurting the Christians was right.

The verse that is amazing in this reading today is verse 4. *Those who had been scattered went about preaching the word.* Paul had caused great sadness for the Christians and many had to leave their homes. You'd think they would have been quiet about Jesus now. Not so. Instead they preached about Him everywhere. They sure must have been convinced Jesus Christ was *the way, the truth, and the life.*

Are you?

JANUARY 7   ACTS 8:9-24

Simon was a magician. The people who saw him thought his power came from God. But it didn't. When Philip came to preach Jesus Christ, Simon believed and was baptized. Now Simon wanted to continue his old ways using God's power to do even greater things. What did Peter say to him about this idea in verse 20?

Simon was a Christian but he didn't want his life to change. He still wanted to do the things he used to. But that was not what God wanted for him. When a person becomes a child of God's his life should become different. Perhaps not suddenly, but gradually. Day by day the change should be seen more clearly as God makes His child more like His Son Jesus Christ.

Is this change happening in your life or are you, like Simon, trying to still do things your way?

JANUARY 8   ACTS 8:25-31

Philip was told exactly what to do by God and he did it. First he was to go on a special trip and then he was to talk to a certain person. Both times he obeyed God's Word. Philip didn't decide for himself that the court official would not want to be bothered. He went right to him because God told him to.

You and I don't usually hear God speaking to us as Philip did. But God has told us many things in His Word that we are to do. Do we do them or do we make excuses? For example, do we respect and obey our Moms and Dads? Or can we think of a hundred reasons why this command doesn't apply to us?

JANUARY 9   ACTS 8:32-40

Here is a dramatic but simple example of a person becoming a Christian. God's Word was used to explain Christ. Philip didn't say a lot about his own experience. He simply taught the eunuch about Jesus from the Bible. God was able to speak through this and as soon as the eunuch saw water he wanted to be baptized. Baptism is to follow the new birth into God's family. When a person becomes a Christian he is then baptized. So Philip gladly baptized the eunuch after he trusted in Jesus. That was the end of Philip's job at that time.

God was able to use Philip to bring someone to Himself because of his obedience. Obedience is very important in God's eyes.

JANUARY 10   ACTS 9:1-9

Saul was a man who believed in God and wanted to please Him. By putting the Christians to death he thought he was doing God's will. They had spoken out against the Jewish laws. But Saul didn't understand that Jesus, God's Son, had come to free the people from all their law burdens. Now Jesus Christ had spoken to him personally. He sees his mistake. What will he do?

Maybe you have tried to please God all your life. You've gone to church and tried to be good. At camp this summer you heard about Jesus Christ and His death. This is God's way. He wants to free you from your sin. Will you accept God's way instead of continuing to try your own?

JANUARY 11   ACTS 9:10-16

When a surgeon goes in to operate on a patient he chooses a very special knife. Your mom's butter knife may be fine to spread your bread but the doctor certainly wouldn't use it, would he? Each knife has a special use.

A milk jug is great for milk but not so good to carry eggs in. You wouldn't want to carry milk in an egg carton either.

"He is a chosen instrument (or vessel) of mine" (verse 15). God chooses special people for special jobs. God had a particular job for Saul and for Ananias. What were they?

God also has a job for you, no matter who you are or what you look like. Ask Him what He wants you to do today.

JANUARY 12   ACTS 9:17-22

No one could understand the change in Saul. They were amazed. He had killed the Christians for talking about Jesus before and now he was preaching about Him. Do you see what Saul did as soon as he became a Christian? Verse 20 tells us that immediately he began to talk about Jesus. The more he talked about Jesus to others, the stronger he became.

"I stand before the cross of Christ,
The Saviour crucified,
And love repeats in whisper low:
T'was in my place He died.

Unworthy of such mighty love,
I stand without a plea;
But when His justice marks my guilt,
I cry: He died for me.

He took my place, my soul is free.
The price has all been paid.
On Him that day upon the tree
My guilt and sins were laid."

Helen Sylvester

JANUARY 13   ACTS 9:23-31

Saul had become a Christian. Now he was in constant trouble. The Jews wanted to kill him and the Christians wouldn't trust him. But he was so sure that Jesus Christ was alive that he spoke out anyway. You might think he'd have been better off staying quiet. Saul was more concerned for other people than he was for his own life. He knew that unless they heard of Jesus they couldn't please God at all. He could see so many others who were just like he had been. He had to preach about Jesus Christ.

Do you know Jesus Christ in this way? Is He so important to you that you want others to know Him too?

JANUARY 14   ACTS 9:32-43

Read today's passage. Cover the answers until you have tried the questions.

1. What two people were healed by God's power?
   Aeneas and Dorcas
2. Who was paralyzed for eight years?
   Aeneas
3. Why was Dorcas raised from the dead?
   The widows wanted her alive again.
4. Why did the women love Dorcas?
   She was always kind and did many good things.
5. What happened as a result of these two miracles?
   Many people believed on the Lord Jesus Christ.

Did you get them all right? I hope so.

JANUARY 15   ACTS 10:1-8

Prayers and alms. That's what God remembered when He thought about Cornelius. Cornelius enjoyed talking to God a great deal. But he didn't just pray. He did something to show God he really meant what he said. Cornelius gave alms. This could mean several things, like giving money to the church or doing good and kind things for others.

Cornelius knew that "actions speak louder than words." He showed God that he was serious. How do you show God you mean business with Him? What outward way do you have of expressing your inner feelings about God?

Project: Make a list of things you might do to show God you really are serious about pleasing Him.

JANUARY 16   ACTS 10:9-18

Does God love you more than the worst person in your class? Maybe you wouldn't come right out and say that but maybe you really think He does.

Peter thought God loved only Jews. One day he had a dream. In it God told Peter that he must not think that any more. God loves everyone in just the same amount, even those who weren't Jews. Peter had to learn that. If we are very good for a while and try our best to please God, we think He must love us more then. But that is not His kind of love. That's our kind of love. We love people more if they are nice to us but God's love is always the same - for everyone. Isn't that a wonderful kind of love?

> God's love is like a circle,
> A circle big and round;
> For when you see a circle,
> No ending can be found.
> And so the love of Jesus
> Goes on eternally.
> For ever and for ever
> I know that God loves me!

JANUARY 17   ACTS 10:19-33

One day, walking home from school, John and Steve spotted Mary playing ball beside her house. "That Mary," said Steve, "She thinks because she's a Christian she's better than anybody else."

Sad to say, this is heard too many times about Christians. A Christian *should* act in a way that would please God. But others should see Jesus in a Christian's life, not just a person trying to be very good.

Peter made sure that Cornelius saw God and not himself, didn't he? (Read verse 26.) Now Peter could preach Jesus Christ to him instead of a "good Peter"! Don't want other people to copy *you* but rather want them to be like *Jesus*.

JANUARY 18   ACTS 10:34-48

Think of who you would want to go and tell about Jesus. Do you pick out friends who would make good Christians? Maybe those who are kind and loving or those who are obedient at school and at home? We know what a Christian should be like so we try and help God a little by picking out someone who is pretty good already.

God doesn't need that kind of help. He doesn't use our method of choosing people who need Him.

Peter was sent to preach to people he would never have chosen. These were people who needed to hear about Jesus Christ. God knew that. When they heard, they acted right away because God, not Peter, had chosen them.

JANUARY 19   ACTS 11:1-18

How do you become a prince or a princess? Can you apply for the position or buy the title? Of course not. There is only one way to become a member of a royal family. You must be born into it.

The Jews were very upset when Peter told them that Gentiles (anyone who isn't a Jew) were also receiving God's Spirit. They had been born into God's chosen race and thought God's favour was limited to them. Now Peter was telling them this was no longer true. God had sent Jesus Christ to die so that anyone who trusted in Him could become His child by adoption. Many Gentiles were believing and receiving the Holy Spirit.

Are you in God's royal family? You have this privilege just as they did in Peter's day.

JANUARY 20   ACTS 11:19-30

Many people believed and began to follow the teachings of Jesus Christ. Barnabas and Saul had classes for these beginning Christians to show them the new way.

Once you accept Jesus Christ as your Saviour you are at the beginning of a new life. Now you start to learn each day a little of what God wants to teach you. Sometimes you learn by reading your Bible or by listening to other Christians. Remember that God wants you to become like your Saviour, Jesus Christ. But you will not go to bed one night and wake up the next day being just like Him. It will take time. As you allow God to change you, you will gradually become more like Him.

As one person said after another failure, "Please be patient with me, God isn't finished with me yet."

JANUARY 21   ACTS 12:1-10

Somehow God's power is set into motion by our prayer. Today's story about Peter is an exciting one. It is also a tremendous example of what prayer can do. The whole church of Christians were praying that God would act for Peter. And God did act. Peter hardly believed what was happening to him. He thought he was dreaming. Have you ever had a prayer answered that you could hardly believe? We forget easily who God is, don't we? When we forget, we lose sight of the real power prayer can be.

If your school friend gave you a cheque for $10,000, would you run to the bank and cash it? Not likely! But if the Prime Minister gave you the cheque instead, you'd cash it right away. What is the difference? The person who stands behind the cheque.

In the same way when you know the Person who stands listening to your prayer, you can pray and expect answers.

JANUARY 22   ACTS 12:11-19

Do you expect God to answer your prayers? What are you talking to God about today? Will you be ready for His answer?

The church was really praying for Peter. They were very sad to have him in prison where he was badly treated. They had talked to God so much about him. Now he was at their front door instead of in jail. But they couldn't believe God had really answered their prayer, could they? They even told poor Rhoda that she was crazy. When they saw Peter they were completely surprised. They had forgotten that God is a God of miracles.

And He is still the same today!

JANUARY 23   ACTS 12:20-25

"... and he did not give God the glory"

King Herod did not offer God any praise or honour for what He had done. He was very angry about Peter's escape and would not think that God had anything to do with it.

If we are Christians we should look for God's action in

everything. Nothing happens in our lives by mistake. We are to thank God every day even if things seem to go wrong. Our lives should *always* give God glory or praise, not just when good things happen to us.

JANUARY 24   ACTS 13:1-12

Paul and Barnabas, after praying and fasting (not eating for several meals), went on a missionary trip. They found a man called Bar-Jesus who didn't believe in Christ. He wasn't satisfied with his own unbelief. He wanted others around him to disbelieve also. He tried to keep his friend, a government official, from believing in Christ. (Read verse 8 again.)

Maybe you would like to become a Christian. Perhaps you have almost made that decision at one time but some person kept you back. So you didn't come to Jesus Christ.

There will always be one excuse or another for not becoming a Christian. Don't let other people keep you away from Jesus. He loves you more than anyone on earth ever could.

JANUARY 25   ACTS 13:13-25

Read today's passage and then see how well you can answer the questions. Cover the answers as you read, then look to check.

God's chosen people were the Israelites. Out of this Jewish people God had promised a Saviour. He would be an Israelite. King Saul and King David would be his ancestors. Paul was telling the people that Jesus Christ was this man, their Messiah.

1. God's Saviour would be an _____.
   [*Israelite*]
2. This means He would be of the _____race.
   [*Jewish*]
3. His ancestors were to be _____ and _____.
   [*King David   King Saul*]
4. This Jewish Messiah was_____.
   [*Jesus Christ*]

JANUARY 26   ACTS 13:26-37

Many hundreds of years before Jesus came to earth the Psalms were written by David. He told things about the Jews' Saviour, or Messiah. One of these Paul points out in today's reading. God's Son, who would be the Saviour, would never decay or rot in the ground as other bodies do. Since God had raised Him from the dead and many people had seen Him, this proved that He was the Jews' Saviour. Even David, a very special person to the Jews, died and decayed as other men do. But not Jesus Christ. He controls death and is more powerful than it. Isn't this a good reason to thank and praise Him today?

JANUARY 27   ACTS 13:38-43

What sins are holding on to you? Make a list of things in your life that are keeping you from loving God above everything else. Perhaps it is one friend who likes to get you into trouble or maybe it is watching too much TV. Anything can cause you to sin if you put it before pleasing God.

Now for the good news. You've likely heard it before. God thought it was so important that this news comes to you again and again in your Bible. What is it? Yes, Jesus came to forgive your sin. Read verse 38. Confess it to Him and then use all your will power to refuse to sin again. Turn off that TV. or find a new friend. It isn't simple, but with God's power and your will power it is wonderfully possible. That is why Jesus came.

JANUARY 28   ACTS 13:44-52

Now for a little test. Read today's passage. Then cover the answers until you've tried the questions.

1. Who were the missionaries in today's reading?
   Paul and Barnabas
2. To whom are they speaking today?
   The Jews
3. Who were coming to believe in Jesus Christ?
   The Gentiles
4. Who are the Gentiles?

Anyone who isn't a Jew

5. Why did Paul and Barnabas leave the area?

*The Jews were angry and drove them
out of the district.*

How well did you do? All five right? Good for you!

JANUARY 29   ACTS 14:1-7

One great gift you have is the gift of choice. You make many choices every day. What cereal you like best, whether to wear a red top or blue, whom to walk home from school with, may be some of your choices. You also may choose whether to do right or wrong. God gave you this power of choice or free will.

In today's reading there were two groups of people who chose two different ways. Some sided with the Jews against Jesus Christ and others agreed with the disciples. You are asked to make this choice every day, even after you become a Christian. Are you living for God or against Him by your thoughts and actions?

JANUARY 30   ACTS 14:8-18

Paul was speaking to Gentiles who worshipped a number of man-made gods. When he made a lame man walk, they thought Paul must be one of these gods. Why did Barnabas and Paul tear their robes and get very upset at this? Read verse 15.

Their whole reason for living was to bring praise and people to God, wasn't it? They didn't want any praise for themselves.

When someone tells you how kind you've been or how helpful you are, it makes you feel good, doesn't it? That is natural. But try to remember that our real reason for being a kind person is to bring glory to God, not to get others to like us. Help them to see Jesus Christ in all the good that you may do.

JANUARY 31   ACTS 14:19-28

Poor Paul! He did all he could for the Lord and yet he always seemed to be getting into trouble. In today's reading the Jews thought they had killed him. Barnabas and he were going from city to city preaching about Jesus Christ and they were always in great danger. This time Paul is stoned and dragged out of the city. You would think he would give up, and go quietly to a place where he could just read the Bible and pray. But no. He goes instead to help other Christians who might be afraid or discouraged. Isn't that great! He sure wasn't a selfish man, was he? That's because Jesus Christ was everything to Paul. He said, "For me to live is Christ."

FEBRUARY 1   ACTS 15:1-12

If someone were to ask how to become a Christian, what would your answer be? Go to church, read the Bible, be good, obedient, don't swear, or cheat, or steal? Is that God's way? What were certain men from Judaea saying (verse 1)? Is this God's way? No it isn't (verse 11). *Nothing* we can do can save us! Jesus Christ has done it all, He became God's perfect sacrifice for sin. We need to believe this and accept His gift of salvation. This is God's way for everyone. What is your answer to Him?

FEBRUARY 2   ACTS 15:13-35

Sometimes it's difficult to keep from doing something we know is wrong. Perhaps friends try to persuade us, and we almost give in. The Christians in Antioch, Syria and Cilicia were listening to people and doing what they wanted. They forgot to listen to what God wanted. Sounds like us. Like them, we too need to be reminded of what God says. Let's not tune out.

FEBRUARY 3   ACTS 15:36-41

Sounds as though Paul and Barnabas had an argument - at least a disagreement. They didn't end their friendship, but reached a solution that brought great results. God's way is the best. Paul went one way, Barnabas the other, and more people heard about the Lord Jesus. Are we sticking so closely to our friends that others around us don't hear about Him? Are you willing, like Paul, to go alone and share Christ with others?

FEBRUARY 4   ACTS 16:1-12

Most of us want to do something for God. If we are really honest, we want to do it in our own way. Paul and young Timothy were God's servants. They too wanted to do something for God. God had changed their lives, and now they wanted to be obedient to Him. They tried to continue on their journey, but God said, "No." They listened, and were obedient to the Lord. God speaks to each of us in different ways - through His Word, prayer, people, circumstances. Each of us can know what He wants. Today, let's ask the Lord what He wants, and let's be obedient servants.

FEBRUARY 5   ACTS 16:13-24

Are you happy? Probably your answer is yes, but think again. If everything you had were removed, would your answer still be yes? Paul had left everything to follow Christ. He was constantly moving. His happiness did not depend on things or people, but *on his walk with God.* He constantly talked to Him in prayer. Sometimes we are so busy doing things that we have no time to read or pray. But in the quiet moments alone with God, we learn the secret of being really happy. We learn what God is like, and all that He wants to be to us. We learn about ourselves and what God wants us to be. Even in Paul's busy schedule he took the time to talk to the Lord. What does your happiness depend on?

FEBRUARY 6   ACTS 16:25-40

"It's not fair! I don't deserve that! I didn't do anything wrong! Boy, would I ever like to get even with him!" Sound like us when we are being blamed for something? We want to react and get even! What would we be like if we were in Paul's position? Things really look tough, but the result is great! The keeper of the prison and his family trusted the Lord Jesus Christ as their Saviour, and became members of God's family. God says, "Blessed are those who are persecuted for righteousness' sake; for theirs is the kingdom of heaven" (Matthew 5:10). How we react to things that are tough really counts. How are you reacting today?

FEBRUARY 7   ACTS 17:1-9

Paul and Silas were accused of turning the world upside down (verse 6). They were being accused of creating disturbance and causing riots. But, was that what was really happening? Many people who heard Paul preach that Jesus Christ is the Messiah believed. Some of these people held important positions in the town. Other Jewish leaders were jealous and afraid of what was happening and so accused them. You see, they saw lives changed because of Jesus Christ. Paul and Silas knew Jesus Christ and wanted to share Him with everyone. Yes, the world was being turned upside down, not with disturbance and riot, but by God's message. What about our world - the place where we live - our home, our neighbourhood? How much of it has been turned upside down because we want everyone to know that Jesus Christ, God's Son, brings us LIFE?

FEBRUARY 8   ACTS 17:10-15

Have you ever tried to walk across the top of a fence? For a few steps it's easy to balance, but then it becomes more difficult, and possibly we even fall. We can fall only to one side, not both. We can't "ride the fence" in our relationship to God either. We are either on His side or not. The only way to keep on His side is to "search daily and receive with readiness His Word." What side are you on? "Thy word have I hid in mine heart, that I might not sin against Thee" (Psalm 119:11).

FEBRUARY 9   ACTS 17:16-34

Look about you. You have a nicely furnished bedroom, a roof over your head, lots to eat, people who provide for you, freedom to choose, friends, opportunities for fun and... Has your thinking gone deeper than just what you have? Do you wonder where it all comes from, or are you too busy complaining about what isn't there? Paul had a great chance to share with the philosophers. Here is one of the things he said we *all* need to think about: "In Him (Jesus Christ) we *live* and *move,* and *have our being.*" Apart from God there would be nothing. He gives us life, the ability to live, and new life by the forgiveness of our sins. Let's check our attitudes today. Are we thankful for all that God has given us?

FEBRUARY 10   ACTS 18:1-8

HRRMPH!

What a sad picture! Time after time people were told that Jesus Christ, God's Son, had come to show us how much God loves us. He became the Sacrifice for our sin. But, as *we* sometimes do, people didn't listen. They laughed, they scorned, they blasphemed. Paul had witnessed to them. He had done what God wants. The people had to choose and they chose no. Perhaps you are like that. Parents, friends, teachers try to warn us, but we listen only when it is too late. Today, let's ask the Lord to help us to listen and choose correctly.

FEBRUARY 11   ACTS 18:9-17

When people don't seem to understand, when the pressure is on, our reaction is to give up. After all, we have tried everything and it still doesn't work. As God encouraged Paul to keep on, He encourages us. He knows exactly what we're going through. When we are doing what is right and things still are tough, remember His Word: "Don't be afraid, for I am with you, and no one can harm you." He, the unchanging God, is with us. Hang in there!

FEBRUARY 12   ACTS 18:18-28

Let's take a look at what Paul was really like. People, many people were against him and what he was saying. His life was threatened, he was beaten. Whom did he think of? Not himself, but those with whom he was working. What an example of the unselfishness of God! Even when things were tough, he encouraged and helped peopie grow in the Lord. Let's thank the Lord today for people who, in spite of everything that is happening to them, spend time encouraging us and helping us grow.

FEBRUARY 13   ACTS 19:1-12

John the Baptist had prepared the way for Christ's coming. When John baptized, it showed that people wanted to turn from their sin to God. John's work prepared. The Lord Jesus finished the work. He is the *Way* through which we can turn from sin to God. To be a member of a church, to be baptized is not enough. Jesus says, *"I am the Way, the Truth, and the Life: no man cometh unto the Father, but by me"* (John 14:6). Do you know Jesus Christ as your Saviour?

FEBRUARY 14   ACTS 19:13-20

Whom do you try to fool most? Your parents, friends, God? Whom are you really fooling? Only yourself. Seven sons of Sceva, chief of the priests, tried very much to do what Paul did. Why couldn't they? Simply, because they did not know

God, and God couldn't work through them. They were trying to bring shame to Paul and dishonour to God. But what happened? No one was fooled. People recognized as never before who God is. They worshipped Him. They understood that God knows us inside out. They saw that what Paul said concerning Him was Truth, and they trusted in Him. What about you? Are you playing games with God?

FEBRUARY 15   ACTS 19:21-41

Year after year styles change. Some business people lose a lot of money because of this. The same thing happened many, many years ago. The reasons were different, however. People were no longer interested in worshipping idols. They wanted to worship the true God, so there was no further need for idols. What a lot of noise Demetrius and the other silver-smiths made! There was almost a riot. The Ephesians yelled about how great the goddess Diana was. The whole

assembly became confused. Their words meant nothing. Those who preached about Jesus Christ were doing nothing wrong - they weren't robbers, nor did they blaspheme the goddess Diana. They shared God's message of salvation and people chose His way. Styles change. God's message doesn't. It is, and always shall be, the same. Are you moving with the latest fad? Or are you trusting in the God who doesn't change?

FEBRUARY 16   ACTS 20:1-12

Do you know how much time each day you spend watching television, talking on the telephone, or just doing nothing? Two hours, three hours? But when we are in church, or

listening to someone speaking about God, we fidget and allow
our minds to wander if they talk more than 20 minutes. Why
does that happen? Is it because we are not really interested?
Too many other things are more important? Notice how long
people wanted to hear about the Lord - all night! Yes - all
night they were eager to hear God's Word. Let's look at
ourselves. How much does God really mean to us? How much
are we really interested in Him?

FEBRUARY 17   ACTS 20:13-24

The Lord Jesus carried His cross toward Calvary, knowing what lay ahead for Him. Paul, urged by the Holy Spirit,
was going toward Jerusalem, knowing that jail and suffering
lay ahead. Each chose to be obedient to the Father. Yes, even
when God's plan meant agony, suffering, and death, neither
turned from God's way. How much do *you* value your life? Can
you say as Paul said, "But *life is worth nothing unless* I use it
for doing the work assigned me by the Lord Jesus - the work
of telling others the Good News about God's mighty kindness
and love" (verse 24)? Are you being the person God wants
you to be? Are you turning from what God asks you to do?

FEBRUARY 18   ACTS 20:25-38

Suppose you had one day to live. What would your last
words be to your friends? Read Paul's last words to the
people of Ephesus again. He had nothing to be ashamed of.
He had done what God wanted. Yes - he could say, "I am
innocent of the blood of all men." He didn't run from
opportunities God gave him to share about Christ, he didn't
say one thing and live another. He had shared the Good News
with *all men*. He could not be held responsible for anyone
turning from God. Now go back to the first question. Would
your last words be making up for lost time?

FEBRUARY 19   ACTS 21:1-9

If you had a map, you would notice all the places where
Paul preached. He always had time to spend with people
wherever he was. He stayed with them long enough to know
their trust was in God. He came back to them to challenge

and encourage them. We become excited when people we
know become interested in the Lord Jesus. We might even
invite them to church, or camp. But soon we forget about
them, and they too lose interest, especially concerning the
Lord Jesus. We need to continue to encourage. Let's not go
part way in our witness. We must do a complete job in
everything. God has not gone just part way with us.

FEBRUARY 20   ACTS 21:10-19

Our parents and friends want and try to protect us from
so many things. They don't want to see us harmed or hurting.
Paul's friends tried so hard to keep him where he was. You
see, they too knew that jail and hardship lay ahead. Do you
remember Paul's last words to the people of Ephesus? He
was ready for *anything*. God's purposes cannot be upset. Although it was very difficult to see him leave, they knew it
was God's way. God does not make mistakes. Let's not hinder
God in His work. He is God. He knows all things.

FEBRUARY 21   ACTS 21:20-29

When someone accuses you of something, do you want to
defend yourself and prove to them they are wrong? People
had been telling the Jewish Christians that Paul was teaching
against God's Law. That was not true. Paul didn't need to say
a word, but by his actions he too showed that he was keeping
the Law. Truth proves itself. Let's walk in truth - His truth.
His truth needs no defense.

FEBRUARY 22   ACTS 21:30-40

Some Jewish people thought that Paul had defiled the
temple of God (verse 29) by bringing some Gentile people
into it. This was against Jewish teaching and caused a mob
reaction, so much so, that people were ready to pull Paul limb
from limb. There was mass confusion. The soldiers heard the
noise and the chief captain came to the rescue. Paul surprised
him by speaking to him in Greek. The chief captain had
assumed Paul was the Egyptian that had caused a riot three
years before, but Paul assured him that he, a Jew, had every
right to be in the temple. There were many, many people

there. Paul asked to speak to them, and he was given freedom to do so. Those who were ready to kill him were silent as Paul began to speak to them. What a tremendous opportunity! Paul used every chance given to witness. Do you?

FEBRUARY 23   ACTS 22:1-10

When we come to a crossroads, we have to decide which way to go. Sometimes that is difficult, especially if we don't really know where we are going.

Life has many crossroads. Each involves a choice. Choice brings consequences. Paul came to a crossroads in his life - one that completely changed him. He had to choose between going God's way or his own. On his own way, he had been doing everything he could to make life miserable for the Christians. When he came to God's crossroads, he chose to follow God. God changed his life. How many times have you come to God's crossroads? What choice have you made? Let's be serious with God. His way leads to life, our way to death.

FEBRUARY 24   ACTS 22:11-21

God had a very special plan for Paul's life. It involved Paul giving up his own plans and allowing God to work out His plans. We make plans for our lives - plans for today, tomorrow, next year, plans that *we* want. Have you ever thought of what God wants for you? God wanted Paul to be His witness to *all* men. Remember what Paul said, "I am innocent of the blood of all men." Paul had fulfilled God's plan. Are you willing to give up your plans? Are you willing to be the person God wants you to be?

FEBRUARY 25   ACTS 22:22-30

It was said of Daniel that he purposed in his heart not to sin against God. Paul also chose to follow God's way, even when many, many people were against him. Each chose to honour God. God says, "...for those who honour Me, I will honour, and those who despise Me will be lightly esteemed" (1 Samuel 2:30). Because Paul chose first in his heart to be obedient to God, God blessed him. Paul's choice didn't mean that everything would be easy (look what happened to him in today's reading) but it did mean that God was free to honour him as He wanted. If we don't honour God, how can we expect God to honour us? What have you made up your mind to do today?

FEBRUARY 26   ACTS 23:1-10

If someone were to ask you why you believed in God, could you give an answer? Paul could. He was not afraid to share what God had taught him. He did not "water down" the Truth. His honesty cost him something. People disliked him, he was put in prison, his life was threatened. Yet, that did not stop him. Because of his desire to share the Truth, people all over the world learned to know God. Let's live *boldly* for Jesus Christ.

FEBRUARY 27   ACTS 23:11-22

God's Word says, "If God be for us, who can be against us?" Many people tried to kill Paul - but that wasn't God's plan. Who would think that a young boy who overheard a conversation would be God's instrument in working out His plan for Paul. This young lad could have forgotten what he heard; the chief captain could have ignored him. But, God was in control. We can trust Him with every part of us. Let's thank Him that His Word is truth. Let's not *doubt* His way.

FEBRUARY 28   ACTS 23:23-35

In the letter to Felix, Lysias stated that Paul had nothing laid to his charge worthy of death or of bonds. In a court of law, he was not guilty. In God's court, would there be enough evidence to convict us? What about when we cheated on that test, or told that little white lie, or thought something wrong? That's different, you say? Or is it? Anything that goes against God's way is sin! Yes, anything! What are you doing about the sin in your life? Jesus Christ grants us forgiveness. What we choose to do about that brings consequences. If we say we know Jesus Christ as our Saviour, then one day we will stand before God and give an account of what we have done for Him. If we don't know Him, we will be punished for our sin. Do we know God's forgiveness so that nothing can be laid to our charge?

MARCH 1   ACTS 24:1-13

If you have been reading The Looking Glass every day, you will know that Paul has been in a lot of trouble for preaching. In verses 5 and 6 we read that they were accusing him of turning the Jews against the government, of being a leader of this new religion and of misbehaving in the temple which was their place of worship. All of these things were untrue - they were just trying to get him out of the way so that he wouldn't preach any more.

Sometimes people will blame us for things we haven't done just because we are Christians. Turn to Matthew 5:11, 12. How should we respond to these people? What do we have to look forward to?

MARCH 2   ACTS 24:14-27

The Bible tells us (1 Peter 3:15) that we should always be ready to tell people why we believe what we do. Paul practiced this even when he was on trial. He used every chance he could get to tell people about Jesus.

Felix was governor at the time and during the trial he became very interested in what Paul was saying. Later on he and his wife called for Paul to come and tell them about his faith. Many people want to hear about Jesus but very few believe. Did Felix believe? Have you believed? Perhaps like Felix you will think that you will wait. Don't wait! We don't read that Felix ever believed. If you wait you may never have another chance.

MARCH 3   ACTS 25:1-11

I don't know about you, but I think this is an exciting story! Here is Paul in the middle of all this trouble yet being able to talk to the rulers of his country. This wouldn't have happened if Paul were not suffering this way.

Suffering is a very necessary part of the Christian life. Through suffering God makes us into the kind of people that He wants us to be.

Felix left Paul in jail until the new governor, Festus, arrived on the scene. During this time Paul told the guards and all the other prisoners about Jesus.

MARCH 4   ACTS 25:12-21

You and I are like balls of clay that are being made into a useful object. God is the Potter and He knows exactly how to make us so that we will be useful. When a pot is being made, some of the clay is removed bit by bit in order to make the pot perfect.

Some of the things that God wants to take out of our lives are selfishness, greed and disobedience, and He wants to give us love, peace and joy.

Even though we think of Paul as a great man of God, he was just like us and needed things taken out of his life. Because God was doing this, Paul was having a chance to even talk to the king about Jesus.

MARCH 5   ACTS 25:22-27

Look up Psalm 119:46. How did David say that he would feel if he had a chance to speak to a king? Now look up Romans 1:16. How does Paul feel about the Gospel? Fill in the blanks: "For I am not _____ of the gospel of Christ; for it is the _____ of God unto _____."

Have you ever been ashamed about someone? You don't want to have anything to do with them, do you? The gospel isn't like that...it is powerful and can bring salvation to people who need it.

I hope you looked up Romans 1:16. The words for the blanks are: ashamed, power and salvation. Memorize that verse today.

MARCH 6   ACTS 26:1-11

Did you memorize Romans 1:16 yesterday? Repeat it to someone today.

Today we read that Paul begins to tell the king about his past life and how he became a Christian. You can read more about it in Acts 9. From this you can see that God can save anyone - no matter how bad they have been.

More than that, God takes a life and remakes it into something useful - like that pot that we talked about on March 4. Paul went from punishing Christians to being one of their leaders and feeding them with the Word of God.

Are you letting God remake you? What will your life be like a year from now - or in ten years? Ask God today to help you to be really useful to Him.

MARCH 7   ACTS 26:12-20

Many of you became Christians at camp last summer. Do you remember the day or night? Was it after a campfire? Or quiet time in your cabin? Or during an activity period? Have you told anyone yet?

Jesus said, "If anyone publicly acknowledges Me as his friend, I will openly acknowledge him as My friend before My Father in heaven" (Matthew 10:32).

Notice that Paul called Jesus "Lord" (verse 15). Before He can really do anything with us we need to call Him "Lord" or "Master". This means that we give Him control of our lives and allow Him to do what He wants with us.

MARCH 8   ACTS 26:21-32

Do your friends ever laugh at you and tell you that you're crazy for being a Christian? This is what Festus told Paul. He said, "Paul, you've learned so much, you're crazy!" Most people don't understand what it means to be a Christian or why Christians think the way they do.

King Agrippa was another one of those people who heard the gospel but, as far as we know, he never became a Christian.

Many young people have said to me, "You have almost convinced me to be a Christian." Almost is not enough! If you almost passed a test at school this week, that means you failed. Are you almost convinced to be a Christian? Why not become fully convinced and believe in Jesus as your Saviour and Lord?

MARCH 9   ACTS 27:1-10

Today we begin one of the most exciting sea adventures recorded in Scripture. Does your Bible have maps in the back? If so, look for the one that shows the journeys that Paul made. This is his last trip and it starts at Caesarea. Paul and other prisoners and their guards set out to go to Rome to see the Emperor. Can you follow the route as it is explained in these ten verses - that's about 800 miles!

What three towns did they land at? Name two islands that they sailed past. How do you think Paul felt? Excited? Scared? Lonely?

As we read on we will see how God protected him on the trip. Get your life jacket ready - this is going to be a rough trip!

MARCH 10   ACTS 27:11-32

This trip began in October and Paul warned the ship's crew that they should spend the winter at Fair Havens. The men wanted to go to Phoenix, about 50 miles away, for the winter and so they left Fair Havens. As you know, they got caught in a terrible storm that lasted over two weeks!

In the middle of it all, God told Paul that He would look after him and that he would live.

This storm reminds me of our lives. Sometimes things get really rough. We get sick, or maybe our Mom or Dad dies, or our parents get a divorce. Does God forget about us? Never! He will always be with us and look after us.

MARCH 11   ACTS 27:33-44

I hope that as you read this you were able to picture the scene in the boat as the men realized that the back of the ship was being smashed and the ship was beginning to sink! I wonder how Paul felt? Was he scared? Or do you think he remembered the promise God gave him. Do you remember? Read verse 24 again.

Did God forget? Of course not! Every promise that God makes to us, He will keep.

Before you finish today, make a list of some things God has promised you and that you know He will make sure you get.

MARCH 12   ACTS 28:1-10

There are at least four ways in which God looked after Paul that are recorded in this passage. What are they?

I remember being on a canoe trip and having a very hard day of paddling. It was almost dark before we found a place to stay. The warm fire, our tents and the pot of hot stew on the fire were our sign that God was really looking after us.

We don't have to be in a ship wreck to see God at work. Everything that we have comes from God...our food, our clothing, our parents and friends are all from Him. When you sit down for your next meal, give God special thanks for all that He has given you.

MARCH 13   ACTS 28:11-21

Are you still following the map to see where Paul is going? After he left the island of Malta or Melita, what three towns did he stop at before finally getting to Rome? The trip from Caesarea to Rome was about 2000 miles...and it took them about five months to make the trip!

Have you noticed that all along the way Paul is using every opportunity to tell others about Jesus? They stayed at Malta for three months and during that time many came to him and were healed after he prayed for them.

We should never let anything keep us from telling others about Jesus. Even when we are sick or in trouble, God wants us to let others know how great He is.

MARCH 14   ACTS 28:22-31

This brings us to the end of Acts. I hope you have learned a lot about how Christianity grew in the years after Jesus went back to heaven.

I have been amazed at the change in Paul since he became a Christian. Remember how he used to carry out orders to punish the Christians? Now he is being punished for being one of their leaders!

Even though he is being guarded, Paul was able to live in a house and have people come and visit him and receive teaching. God wants to do unusual things in our lives, but He wants us to be willing to let Him take over. I hope you are learning what it means to make Him Lord of your life.

MARCH 15   AMOS 2:6-12

I know that some passages in the Bible are difficult to read and understand but don't get discouraged...there are some great things to learn in the next few days. Amos was a preacher like Paul except that he preached before Christ came. He was God's messenger to the nation of Israel.

One way that God lets us know how our sin makes Him unhappy is by reminding us how good He has been to us in the past. In verse 10 He reminds them that He brought them out of slavery in Egypt into the Promised Land.

Even after God had been so good, Israel sinned and showed that they had forgotten Him.

MARCH 16   AMOS 3:1-8

This passage today is all about punishment. Sometimes our parents punish us because we have disobeyed them. Likely we get at least one warning and then if we continue to disobey, we are punished.

God is warning the people that they will be punished for their disobedience. He calls them His family and like a true Father, God will punish them for disobeying.

Sometimes God punishes us for disobeying His Word, the Bible, which is full of commands for us to obey. They are there to help us live a happy life. If we disobey, He is not happy and He punishes us.

MARCH 17   AMOS 5:1-14

God really condemns Israel for the way they treat other people. Notice in verse 11 He condemns those who charge heavy rent to people who can't afford to pay it. People who make money in dishonest or unfair ways are displeasing to God and He promises to judge them.

Have you noticed that three times God says, "Seek me and you will live"? Jesus said, "Seek ye first the kingdom of God..." (Matthew 6:33).

To put money and other things first is wrong. We should seek God first and He will give us everything we need. If we do this, Amos says in verse 14 that the Lord will be with us!

MARCH 18   AMOS 7:10-15

Doesn't this sound like Paul? Amos is being accused of speaking against the king and the nation! This gives him the opportunity to talk to the king and to tell him personally what God wants to say.

You see, God works with man in the same way today as He did in the time of Amos and Paul. He never changes.

If you are a Christian, it's because God knew about you a long time ago and He has a special job for you to do. Everything that happens in life is ordered by God and it is so that His plan for the earth will be accomplished.

MARCH 19   JOEL 1:1-7

Joel was another preacher who lived at the same time as Amos. Most of these prophets had a message of judgment to bring to the people - it was a message that God gave them to preach.

Joel is talking about a plague of locusts that had invaded the land and eaten their crops. This was just a sign of what was to come in the future. God would judge the nation by sending armies of other nations to make war with Israel.

To walk with God is a great thing...to experience His love is the most wonderful blessing in the world. This is made possible when we obey all His commands.

MARCH 20   JOEL 2:10-15

Although we have been thinking a lot about judgment, notice how God offers forgiveness in verses 12 and 13.

First we must be sorry for our sin. Sin really makes God sad. He loves us and wants to be our Friend, but sin makes that very difficult.

Second, we must turn away from sin. That means beginning to obey our parents. Some may stop lying...others stop stealing or cheating. But we must leave these things and turn to God.

Verse 13 tells us what God is like. He is loving, forgiving and patient. He will do anything to bring us back to Himself; in fact, that's exactly why Jesus came - to bring us back to God.

MARCH 21   JOEL 2:23-29

Today we will do a little extra reading in the Bible - so get ready. Turn to John 14 and read verses 16 and 17 and then verse 26. In these verses we hear Jesus promising that after He left the earth, He would send His Spirit - the Holy Spirit. Now turn to Acts 2 and read verses 1-21. Do you recognize Acts 2:17-21?

What Jesus promised in John and what took place in Acts 2 are exactly what Joel said would happen! How did Joel know? Because God told him!

This is only one of many times that something is talked about in the Old Testament and then it happens in the New Testament. Things like this help us to believe that the Bible is really God's Word.

MARCH 22   JEREMIAH 1:1-10

Jeremiah was another preacher who brought God's message to Israel *after* Amos and Joel. In this passage today we find out how God called him to be a preacher.

Jeremiah gave God two reasons why he shouldn't serve Him. First he said, "I don't know what to say!", then, "I am too young." What excuses do we give to God today for not obeying Him? List some of them.

I think Jeremiah was afraid of what he would have to do. Look at the promise God gives him in verse 8... "I am with you to deliver you."

Remember that no matter where we are or what we are doing, God is always with us.

MARCH 23   JEREMIAH 17:1-11

In the Old Testament God uses a lot of picture language to teach us. This means that we have to read more carefully in order to understand what He is telling us.

In verses 5-11 God compares two men. One trusts in man and the other trusts in God. Describe the man who trusts in mankind in verse 6...now describe the one who trusts in God.

Who said that He was a fountain of living waters? Jesus did. Now if we trust Him we will be like a tree that is getting all the water it needs to grow.

If our trust is in Jesus Christ, He will give us real life and we will grow up to be men and women whom God will use.

MARCH 24   JEREMIAH 18:1-10

In this passage God shows Jeremiah that Israel is just like a clay pot that is being made. Remember I talked about this on March 4?

When a clay pot is being made, the rough edges are taken off and new pieces of clay are added in order to get it just the way the potter wants it.

Some of the "rough edges" that God is taking off us are dishonesty, greed, selfishness and disobedience. He is adding love, peace, honesty, kindness and many other things to make us the kind of people He wants us to be.

I hope you are letting Him be the Master Potter of your life.

MARCH 25   JEREMIAH 36:1-20

Most of us think that we can sin and God will just let us go on and never punish us. Just because we have invited Jesus into our life doesn't mean that we can continue to sin. Sin means disobeying God. Our parents don't let us away with disobeying them and neither does God.

In verses 2 and 3 we find out how God feels about Israel's sin. He was very angry and was telling the people that they were going to be judged.

As you read the Bible, I hope you understand that all the commands of God are for us today and we must obey them.

MARCH 26   JEREMIAH 36:21-32

Did you notice how angry the king became when the message was read to him? Why do you think he was so angry?

Many people do not like what God has to tell us. God hates sin and in His Word He warns us that sinners will be punished.

The fact is that all of us have sinned (Romans 3:23) and God will one day punish all those who have disobeyed Him.

If you have never asked Jesus to forgive your sin, why not ask Him right now? He really loves you and wants you to confess your sin and invite Him to become the Lord of your life.

MARCH 27   JEREMIAH 37:1-10

WARNING: STRONG UNDERCURRENT. ALL SWIM-MERS MUST WEAR LIFE JACKETS. This sign is posted at the end of the lake near our camp where the water runs out of the lake, over a dam and into the river. Although the sign is large and easily read, every summer people swim there without life jackets on.

What happens? Some of them drown. They are pulled lifeless from the water with the warning sign within sight.

The danger was real...they were warned, but paid the price for not obeying.

Jeremiah had a warning for the king. Would he listen? When God warns us, we should listen and keep ourselves from danger.

MARCH 28   JEREMIAH 37:11-21

Do you remember how the Apostle Paul was put into prison? You see that wasn't a new thing because God's servants were being jailed for doing His work years before Paul began to preach.

Look at 2 Timothy 3:12. God promises us that we will be persecuted if we want to serve Him. Sometimes our friends will laugh, or even our parents may laugh at us. Maybe one of us will be put in jail for being a Christian. Could it be that we might be murdered because we are following Jesus?

I'm sure that during this time in jail, Jeremiah remembered God's promise, "Do not be afraid...I am with you."

MARCH 29   JEREMIAH 38:1-13

For Jeremiah, things seem to go from bad to worse! After telling the people again about God's judgment, Jeremiah is thrown into a well. It was hoped that he would die there. However, his work wasn't finished yet and God made sure that he was rescued from the well.

You see, God has a plan for each of our lives. If you have asked the Lord Jesus to be your Saviour and Lord, then God will protect you and guide you until your work is done... nobody can stop you!

Thank Him today for His love and for the fact that you are His child and nothing can stop you from doing His work.

MARCH 30   JEREMIAH 38:14-28

Again Jeremiah is before the king and is warning him about God's judgment. I'm glad that I didn't have that job!

Jeremiah is known as "The Weeping Prophet". He cried a lot because of the sin of the people and because God was going to judge them.

Jeremiah told the king the truth. You and I also need to warn people about God's judgment if they do not ask for

forgiveness. If we don't warn them, they will never know...
and may die without ever having a chance to tell God that
they're sorry.

When you share your faith, tell people the good things
about becoming a Christian, but don't forget to tell them
what will happen if they do not become Christians.

MARCH 31   JEREMIAH 45:1-5

Baruch was Jeremiah's secretary...he wrote down all the
messages that God gave Jeremiah and read them to the
people.

In this passage God has a message for Baruch. He is
telling him that even though there will be judgment on the
whole land, Baruch's life will be spared and he will be safe.

One day, the Bible tells us, this whole world will be
destroyed. For those of us who have trusted Jesus we will be
safe with God. I hope that you are ready - either for the end
of this age or for the time you die. My friend, don't wait,
but invite Jesus to take over your life today.

APRIL 1   JOSHUA 1:1-9

Moses has died and Joshua is now to lead the people to
the land the Lord had promised to them (verses 3,4). "Every
place that the sole of your foot shall tread upon..." Not only
did God give Joshua the promise of the land, but He also
gave him personal encouragement to help him carry out the
desires of the Lord (verses 7-9). God's promise of salvation is
even greater (John 10:28) and His encouragement to us today
is just as personal (Matthew 28:20b).

APRIL 2   JOSHUA 1:10-18

After the Lord spoke to Joshua telling him that he was to
be the leader of the Israelis, Joshua went before the people to
let them know God's plans. The people listened to Joshua and
then answered him. They not only agreed to do as Joshua
instructed them, but they also gave him personal encouragement (verse 18b, "'...be strong and of a good courage"). Are
there people in your life to whom you can offer encouragement and, as well, receive encouragement from for yourself?

APRIL 3   JOSHUA 2:1-7

In these verses we find Joshua beginning plans to take the people into the land. Let us keep in mind that there were people living in the land that the Israelis were to claim. These people were not ready to just give up their land - so Joshua sent spies into the area to find out what it was like. The spies knew the protection of God through Rahab, a woman who lived in the land. God often uses other people to bring His protection and character building into our lives. Are you taking advantage of the help that is being offered to you even today?

APRIL 4   JOSHUA 2:8-24

The men promised Rahab that she and her family would be spared if she met all the requirements. The requirements were: to let the rope hang down, that it be red in color, that all who were to be saved from disaster must be inside the house, and that she was not to say anything about them or their business. Rahab accepted the conditions of the agreement and they left. Later we shall see if Rahab keeps her part of the bargain and to what extent the men of Israel kept theirs.

APRIL 5   JOSHUA 3:1-8

For the second time since we began reading in Joshua we find where the Lord spoke to Joshua. He speaks again to give him personal encouragement. This encouragement was not to be of a private nature, just between Joshua and God. God tells Joshua that He is going to let all of Israel know that He has chosen Joshua and will guide him just as Moses had been guided. You see, if we are doing those things that God would choose for us to do, He will guide us and let others know that we are doing His business.

APRIL 6   JOSHUA 3:9-17

Remember how the Lord opened up the water for Moses so the people of Israel could cross the Red Sea? Well, the Lord does the same thing in today's reading for Joshua and the people he is leading. How true God is to His promises -

He promised Joshua that He would be with him and God kept His Word. Are you trusting God in the same way that Joshua did? Remember He is an unchanging God!

APRIL 7   JOSHUA 4:1-14

Did you get the thrill and impact of verse 14 in today's reading? The Scripture says, "On that day the Lord magnified Joshua in the sight of all Israel;..." Was this not a part of God's planning in preparing Joshua to do the mighty work he was to do for God? You see, had Joshua tried to take on God's responsibility, he would have failed. It was God's responsibility to bring about God's desires, not Joshua's. God wanted to use Joshua as an instrument. Joshua's responsibility was to be obedient. Do you sometimes try to work out God's plans for you instead of depending on and trusting Him? He is a faithful and capable God. Allow Him to be to you the leader and guide He desires to be.

APRIL 8   JOSHUA 4:15-24

The stones mentioned today were to be a testimony of the power and might of God when He held the waters back. The people were to tell the coming generations of all that God had done. How exciting it must have been to repeat the story again and again! Although, perhaps not any more exciting than to relate that the God of so long ago is still the same God of today. The stones were to be a reminder. We are to be reminders or witnesses to others of the change brought about in our lives through faith in what Jesus did at the cross of Calvary. That was the greatest of all miracles.

APRIL 9   JOSHUA 5:1-9

One of the more significant happenings in the portion today is the circumcisions taking place. However, I would like us to think about verse 6. It is in this verse that we find out why Moses and the others who left Egypt were not allowed to enter the Promised Land. Can you tell why? One word tells it all - disobedience. It is this word that describes how we deprive ourselves so many times of the things God wants us to have and/or be. God wanted the people of Israel to possess the land that He promised to them, but time and time again they chose to do things their own way. Don't cheat yourself out of God's best. Be obedient to His Word and choices for you.

APRIL 10   JOSHUA 5:10-15

God had given Joshua the responsibility of leading His people in war. Canaan was occupied by people who did not worship God, and the small, untrained, poorly equipped army of Israel faced impossible battles against them. Joshua could have been discouraged and afraid upon entering the land. He wasn't. This man stood before Joshua with a sword, accepted his worship (verse 14), and wanted him to recognize His holiness (verse 15). It was the Lord! From that day forward, Joshua knew that God Himself would fight the battles, and he was not alone with his small army. Moses learned the same lesson (Deuteronomy 20:4), as did the kings (2 Chronicles 20:15,17). Read these verses and understand that God is with you to win impossible battles against Satan and sin in your life.

APRIL 11   JOSHUA 6:1-19

I found this portion of Scripture quite fascinating. I've never had to prepare for or plan a battle, but I'm sure if I had been told to do the things Joshua had to do I would have thought it quite strange. After all who ever heard of winning a battle by marching and blowing horns, let alone fighting one in that way. Yet, we do not find Joshua or any of the others hesitating.

We can learn so much from others - whether in the Scriptures
or around us. Are you listening and observing? Learn all you
can from God's people.

APRIL 12   JOSHUA 6:20-27

"...The wall fell down flat...and they took the city"
(verse 20); "and they utterly destroyed all that was in the
city..." (verse 21); "...bring out thence the woman, and all
that she hath..." (verse 22); "And Joshua saved Rahab the
harlot alive..." (verse 25). The battle is over and the Israelis
have won. They fought a strange fight, strange to the ones
who fought, but not strange to the One who laid the plans and
the outcome. That's one of the many advantages that God
has. He does not plan only the battle, but the outcome as
well. And this is to our benefit to have a God such as the
living God. Just try to imagine Joshua's frustrations if he had
to plan the battle, fight, save Rahab, and win the battle too.
He would not have been certain about any part of it. And
think about this: God saved Rahab and all that were with her!

APRIL 13   JOSHUA 7:1-15

The Lord had seen to it that the Israelis were cared for
and what do we read today? "...the children of Israel com-
mitted a trespass...and the anger of the Lord was kindled
against the children of Israel" (verse 1). This often happens
in our lives as born-again Christians. Even when we know
God is taking care of our needs we become selfish and do
things we ought not. Just as God said to Joshua, that in order
to continue to receive further help, the people would have to
be cleansed from their sin. We too can be restored into
proper relationship with God. This can be done if we destroy
the "accursed thing" that is with us. God says to confess
our sins and accept His cleansing (1 John 1:9).

APRIL 14   JOSHUA 7:16-26

It was Achan who sinned and his whole family had to pay
the consequences for his disobedience. It is a sad situation
when we do not stop to realize how our lives and our
behaviour affect others. This is true whether it is in our

families, with our friends, at school, church, wherever. Let us learn to be mindful of others and the influence we can have on them - perhaps even to them becoming, or not becoming, a born-again believer.

APRIL 15   JOSHUA 8:1-13

Once again we read how God gives encouragement to Joshua and another plan to win another battle. Claiming the land that God wanted the Israelis to have was no easy matter. God wanted them to have it; therefore, He told Joshua exactly what to do so that the people could win the battle. To know what will happen before it does - this is God. He knows all things about us. Trust Him to guide your life. Read Psalm 139.

APRIL 16   JOSHUA 8:14-29

Joshua carries out the plans made by God and God is again shown to be a trustworthy God. What do you suppose would have happened had Joshua ignored the plans given to him? Not a pleasant thought, is it? Well, think of the same idea in relationship to yourself. God has plans for your life. If you ignore these plans, be sure you will not have God's blessing. Several times now we have seen the rewards obedience brings. Be obedient and claim your rewards.

APRIL 17   JOSHUA 8:30-35

The Law (the Ten Commandments) was still very important to the people of Israel even though Moses had been dead many years. It was a guide for the people to follow in order that they would know what God had for them. God's complete Word, given so many thousands of years ago, is still very much alive and necessary for us today. It is through God's Word that we can learn who God is, what He has done, what He can do, and what it is He is going to do. We also learn of His love and concern for us as individuals. Read it! Meditate on it! Memorize it! Obey it!

APRIL 18   JOSHUA 9:1-15

We find the Israelis becoming too confident in themselves (verse 14). Because of this over-confidence Joshua and the other leaders are fooled into signing a treaty that never should have been made. How very careless! List the ways the people of Gibeon deceived the Israelis.

APRIL 19   JOSHUA 9:16-27

Joshua and the leaders were tricked; but because they had given their word (verses 18, 19), when the people wanted to attack, they were not allowed to do so. It is difficult, but noble, to stand by one's promise even if it is given when deceived or tricked. Can your word be trusted?

APRIL 20   JOSHUA 10:1-15

Can you believe it? The sun and the moon stood still because of the prayer of one man! (Read verses 13 and 14 again.) The power of prayer should never be taken lightly. Prayer is the Christian's battle weapon. It is through prayer that we not only obtain answers to requests, but it is through prayer that we can know the mind of God and get to know Him to be the mighty God that He is.

APRIL 21   JOSHUA 10:16-27

The Israelis once again realize the reality of the power of God. They have won another battle with very little resistance from the enemy. Joshua reminds them that they should continue to be encouraged because the Lord is going to give them victory over all their enemies (verse 25). You too should be encouraged. God shows His concern for you as you are "casting all your care upon Him; for He careth for you" (1 Peter 5:7).

APRIL 22   JOSHUA 18:1-10

The Israelis are about to claim the land the Lord had promised them. The land was now to be divided among the tribes. The wonderful thing about it all was that each group would receive the right land suited to them. This is the way God works. He always gives us what is right for us. We never have to wonder about it.

APRIL 23   JOSHUA 20:1-9

How would you define the word "refuge"? Now look it up in a dictionary. Were you right? Sometimes we do not understand the Bible because we haven't taken the time to find out the meaning of a word. These cities were places of safety for people who would otherwise have been put to death for accidental murder. It was a special legal provision that God gave to His people in Joshua's day. It reminds me of His provision for us. Jesus Christ is our refuge from God's judgment on our sin. In Joshua's day, a person had to flee to one of these cities in order to be safe. Jesus Christ died for everyone, but I must accept Him as Saviour before I am safe in Him.

APRIL 24   JOSHUA 21:43-45

In today's reading we see how God has completely fulfilled the promises He made to Moses and the ancestors of the Israelis.

"And the Lord gave them peace, just as He had
promised, and no one could stand against them;
the Lord helped them destroy all their enemies.
Every good thing the Lord had promised them

came true'' (Living Bible, verses 44, 45).

WHAT A MIGHTY GOD WE HAVE!

APRIL 25   JOSHUA 22:1-6

Throughout the battles Joshua has remained a loyal leader of his people. Now that the promises of God have been accomplished, he encourages the people to go to their respective homes and enjoy the success and rest that is theirs. As he does so he cautions them to continue to obey all of the commandments; to love the Lord and to follow God's plan for their lives; to cling to Him and serve Him with eagerness (Living Bible). There could be no greater prayer for you if this is the request of your parents, counsellor, or Sunday School teacher. Be thankful that there are people in your life who truly care for you.

APRIL 26   JOSHUA 23:1-9

Joshua realizes that he is getting old and perhaps he will not be leading the Israelis much longer. He takes the time to counsel and remind them not to turn away from the laws even for a moment. He also reminds them how the Lord directed them in battle and on to claiming the land promised to them. We too need to be reminded and it is our responsibility to remind and encourage others.

APRIL 27   JOSHUA 23:10-16

As Joshua admonishes the people of Israel he warns them again that disobedience to the laws of God will only bring heartache. We all know from personal experience that when we disobey any authority we must pay the consequences - so it is with God. God loved the people of Israel, but because He is God they would have to obey His Word before they could receive His blessings. We can turn this thinking to ourselves. God's blessings are ours as we are obedient to Him and His Word.

cop

APRIL 28   JOSHUA 24:1-15

Joshua speaks quite frankly to the Israelis by telling them to make up their minds as to whom they will serve (verse 15). Notice the choice - first he encourages them to serve God (verse 14), but then he says if they find they cannot do so, then they were to make their choice between the false gods of Egypt or the false gods of the Amorites. Joshua states further that, regardless of their choice, he was going to serve the Lord. Do you have that much courage and boldness for God? I trust so.

APRIL 29   JOSHUA 24:16-25

The people make their choice - and their choice is to serve God (verses 18,21,24). The reason for their choice is that they remembered all that the Lord had done for them, from the time of the escape from Egypt through the many battles, to claiming the land promised to them. We can agree that they made a wise decision. Are your decisions relating to God just as wise?

APRIL 30   JOSHUA 24:26-33

Obedience! What a precious testimony, in verse 31, for the people of Israel! They obeyed the Lord. Can this be said of you? Our obedience to God comes in many forms: obedience to parents, teachers, adults, persons in authority, the laws of the land, etc. For in each of these God has directed us to show subjection. As we do so we act as witnesses to our choice to serve the living God.

MAY 1   JUDGES 1:1-7

Butchery! Cruelty! War! These seem so unchristian to us who have been taught much about love in the New Testament. How can God allow, yes, demand such behaviour from His people? And what about those who will live forever in the lake of fire, finding far more pain and suffering than anything written here.

Sin must be punished. God cannot allow sin to increase and not be dealt with. Those living in Canaan had greatly sinned against God and had forsaken Him, so their land was to be taken from them and given to others. Let us learn a lesson from King Adoni-bezek, "as I have done, so God has repaid me." Punishment for sin or blessing for godliness? The choice is yours!

MAY 2   JUDGES 1:8-15

God promised Israel the land of Canaan years before. A quick reading of Joshua and Judges will reveal that He also helped them get it. He gave them battle plans and directions. He gave them strength and power. He even did miracles to help Israel conquer the land. But before Israel could live in the land, they had to get out and fight for it. They never got the land by sitting back and saying, "OK God, go get it for us." The same is true in the Christian life. God has promised much and is willing to do much for us; but to see victory in the Christian life, we must do our part. Live for God and He will come through for you.

MAY 3   JUDGES 1:16-26

The spies moved toward the town. They needed help - a quick and safe way for their army to enter. They asked the help of a man coming out of the town. He helped them and the town was overthrown.

Why do you think this man helped Israel defeat his own people? It was probably for the same reason that Rahab helped Israel overthrow Jericho (Read Joshua 2:1-14.) He saw the Lord helping Israel and knew that no one can fight against God and live, so he came over to God's side.

Do people who know you see God working in your life? Do they desire to become Christians because you are one? Or does your life do more to turn people *away* from God than *to* Him?

MAY 4   JUDGES 1:27-36

We now come to a number of verses that tell us about whom Israel did not conquer - nations that were not driven out of the land. God promised to His people the entire land of Canaan. He told them to drive out *all* the people. They didn't. Don't criticize them too much for we do the same thing. God offers us so much in the Christian life: joy, peace, love, protection, help. But because we're too busy, we let these slip through our fingers. Many Christians today are unhappy, lack purpose in life, are sickly and much more. God has given to us His message in the Bible. Read it! Obey it! Begin to really live.

MAY 5   JUDGES 2:1-10

Remember those nights at camp around the campfire - cooking, singing, keeping warm on a cool evening? Remember how your clothes smelled when you returned to the cabin? They had picked up the odour of the smoke and you carried it with you back to the cabin. The same is true with our life-style. We pick up habits from the people we hang around, the music we listen to, the books we read, the places we go, the things we see. God knew this would happen to Israel. That's why He told them to destroy the people living in Canaan. But they didn't. In a few years they began to act like these other people and worship their idols. They forgot about God who was so good to them. What about you? Do your friends, books, music, the places you go make you more like Christ?

MAY 6   JUDGES 2:11-23

Four statements in this passage summarize the history of Israel during the time of the Judges: 1. "So they forsook the Lord" (verse 13). 2. "He gave them into the hands of plunderers" (verse 14). 3. "The Lord raised up judges to deliver them" (verse 16). 4. "Then they would turn back and act more corruptly" (verse 19). Let's diagram this:

1. *God raises up a judge to deliver them.*

2. *Israel cries to God for help. Judges 3.9.*

3. *In good times Israel returns to sin.*

4. *Israel sins.*

5. *God delivers Israel to their enemies.*

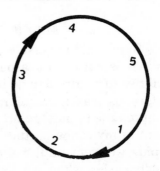

This cycle is repeated throughout the book of Judges. Do you act the same way, forgetting God when everything is great and praying to Him when you are in trouble?

MAY 7   JUDGES 3:1-11

So you made a decision at camp that when you returned home you would live for Jesus. You even prayed to Jesus to give you help; but when you returned home, you found all the problems you had when you left. So you began to wonder, "I prayed, why didn't God take all my problems away?" God knew that Israel would be faced with warlike nations in the future. God prepared them for future problems by giving them smaller ones now. God allows us to have problems that through them we might become the type of people He wants us to be. We will then be able to handle the greater problems we will face in the future.

MAY 8   JUDGES 3:12-31

Did you notice verse 12? It was the Lord who strengthened Eglon. That seems odd, doesn't it? It is the Lord who controls the events of history. Did you think that men controlled their own future? No. It is God who rules on the earth. He puts in power and removes from power those He wants. Today we have enough resources to destroy the world. Isn't it a comfort to know that it is God and God alone who controls what's going to happen. This does not mean that there will be no war, famine, or plagues, for God will punish sin. Live for Christ and let Him take care of the affairs of mankind. Nothing can happen to me unless God wills it.

MAY 9   JUDGES 4:1-10

Barak said in verse 8, "If you will go with me, then I will go." It is natural for a person faced with a task beyond his abilities to be afraid to do it. Once I was on a canoe trip. There before us was a set of rapids. The swiftness of the water tempted me to portage around them, but with the encouragement of my canoe partner we went on. Over and through the rapids we went until we were safe at the other end. Life is much easier when we have friends who will help and encourage us in rough times. If you have no Christian friends then seek some out. Your friends can make the difference between success and failure in your Christian life.

MAY 10   JUDGES 4:11-24

"Arise, for this is the day that the Lord has given Sisera into our hands" (verse 14).

Isn't it great to know that God is on our side? What do we have to fear? What do we have to worry about? Nothing - when we do His will. Barak could have been afraid of 900 iron chariots, he could have been afraid of the large powerful army. But this was God's day and not Sisera's. Today is the Lord's day. He is willing to help us solve today's problems, win today's battles, overcome today's hardships.

Project: List the tasks you have to do today. Think through how God would have you do them. Pray, asking the Lord to help you. Arise and do them.

MAY 11   JUDGES 5:1-11

Ask! Ask! Ask! Ask! It seems that every time we pray we are asking something from God. It is right to ask things of God. The Bible says, "You have not, because you ask not." But God wants us also to praise Him. When we praise God we thank Him for all that He has done for us. We worship Him because He is God and so much greater than we are. After winning the battle, Deborah and Barak wrote this song of praise to God. They wanted all who heard it or read it to know of the great works of God.

Project: List five things that God did for you last week. Right now, thank Him.

MAY 12   JUDGES 6:1-10

This passage says that Israel was "brought very low" (verse 6). Why had it happened? Because they sinned against God (verse 10). Sin never improves a person; it always tears him down. God created us and the world we live in. He knows what is best for us and what will hurt us. Being a loving God, He tells us in the Bible what will hurt us and not be for our profit. The Bible calls this sin. God strongly warns us to avoid it. Instead we should follow His ways for they lead to success and benefit. When God says not to do something, it's not because He is mean. He knows it will hurt us and He doesn't want us to suffer.

MAY 13   JUDGES 6:11-24

What a contrast we have in this passage! The Lord calls Gideon a valiant warrior, but Gideon calls himself a nobody, the youngest member of a small family. Gideon was right, but so was the Lord. Here we see a contrast between what a person is and what he can be if he allows the Lord to shape his life. Are you a nobody? It's probably true, but you can be a great man or woman of God if you follow Him and live according to His way. Here Gideon is hiding in the winepress; later we see him as a general who destroyed the power of the Midianites. God does make a difference.

MAY 14   JUDGES 6:25-32

God had called Gideon to deliver Israel from her enemies. But first there was a problem of sin in his own household. His father had an altar from which he worshipped the false god, Baal. Gideon must destroy it. Do we have sin in our lives which must be removed before God can use us? Are there things which mean more to me than God does, so that I center my life around them and leave God with what is left over?

Gideon was not yet the man of God, God wanted him to be. He destroyed the altar, but at night in secret. Christian growth takes time and before long we find Gideon boldly standing and fighting for his God.

MAY 15   JUDGES 6:33-40

Today is your swimming test at camp. You will be tested to see if you can swim a certain distance. You can't, you failed to practice during camp and so you are doomed to failure. But your instructor holds you up in the water, giving you the strength you need to complete your test.

The above is an attempt to illustrate the work of the Holy Spirit in our lives. God demands that we live by His standards and do what He desires. However, we are unable to do this by ourselves. God gave us the Holy Spirit to live in us when we were saved. A Christian can never fail as long as he allows the Holy Spirit to control his life.

MAY 16   JUDGES 7:1-8

Often the Lord does something for us and we take the credit. "Look how great I am!" Israel had turned from God so often that He again wanted to show to them that He was still God. So often before He had displayed His power, but they had forgotten. When Gideon approached the Midianites with 32,000 soldiers, God said, "too many." "If you win, you'll say your own strength delivered you." Gideon reduced the army to 10,000 and God said, "too many." Once again Gideon reduced the army, to 300. Read verse 12. What are 300 against so many? God wanted Israel to know that it was He, and not they themselves, who would defeat this enemy.

MAY 17   JUDGES 7:9-18

In Old Testament days God often spoke to people through dreams. God used dreams in the Old Testament because most of the Bible was not yet written. Here Gideon is again reassured that he will be victorious though the odds are not in his favour. How does God speak to us today? Today through reading and studying the Bible we learn much of how God desires us to live. We also learn through the advice of others. Your counsellor from camp could give you much advice and so could other mature Christians. God uses many ways to teach us His desires for our lives. He knows that it is to our profit to follow Him.

MAY 18　　JUDGES 7:19-25

To be a Christian does not mean we send our brain on vacation. Notice the wisdom used in the attack on the Midianites:

1. *It was at night.* The surprise and darkness would help the Israelites who were few and carried lights.

2. *It was at the change of the guard.* Those on a later watch would be in a sound sleep. Those who had just left their watch would be moving throughout the camp, so when the others were wakened, they would attack those moving about, thinking they were the enemy (verse 22).

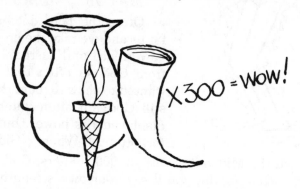

3. *Each Israelite had a torch, pitcher, and trumpet.* To the Midianites, 300 torches, trumpets and all the noise would indicate a much larger force.

From the human viewpoint, Gideon used wisdom but they succeeded because the Lord was at work (verse 22).

MAY 19　　JUDGES 8:1-12

Have you ever noticed that sometimes those who do the least complain the most? Ephraim, probably the most powerful and secure of all the tribes of Israel, did not take the lead to help the rest of Israel overthrow the Midianites. Now the men of Ephraim loudly criticize Gideon, but Gideon put into practice the principle we find in Proverbs 15:1, "A gentle answer turns away wrath, but a harsh word stirs up anger." Gideon used a soft word. He praised the accomplishments of the men of Ephraim and failed to mention any of his own. Let us follow the same example. When we find ourselves being tempted to say something harsh, let's try a soft word.

MAY 20   JUDGES 8:13-21

The latter part of this passage may seem strange to the Christian who has been taught not to seek revenge, but Gideon lived in a different period of history than we do. In Gideon's day (in the absence of central and well organized government), the punishment of crime and the seeking of justice were the responsibility of the person who had been wronged. Today the duty of the Christian is to allow the government to seek justice and to help them, if possible (Romans 13:1-7). A person who has been wronged should not harbour feelings of hate, but should forgive (Matthew 5:43,44).

MAY 21   JUDGES 8:22-35

How quick we are to forget! After the battle is over and the victory is won, the people forgot that it was God who delivered them and not Gideon alone. Rather than returning to worship God, they wanted to make Gideon their king. It was God who was supposed to be their King. God ruled through their priests. When the priests became evil, God raised up judges like Gideon to lead the people of God, but now they wanted a king. Gideon refused. It is so easy to look to people to guide us rather than God. Let us never forget that Christ, and Christ alone, is the Head of the Church and my King.

MAY 22   JUDGES 13:1-14

Meet Samson - probably one of the most famous of all the judges. He is known not because he was a great man of God, but because of the superhuman feats he did during his lifetime.

We might call Samson "the man who might have been." Chosen by God before his birth, he was called to deliver Israel from the oppression of the Philistines. Handsome and powerful, God had well equipped Samson for the job before him. However, Samson was only concerned for himself and lived for the pleasures he might have in the world. He fought the

Philistines, not to deliver Israel, but for personal revenge. He died alone, a prisoner and a failure.

MAY 23　　JUDGES 13:15-25

The Lord, refusing to eat the meal which was offered, asks that it be used for a burnt offering. So the food was placed upon a rock and fire came out of the rock and consumed it. The fire showed that it had been accepted by the Lord.

To give things to the Lord is a way to worship Him. It shows our love and dedication to the Lord. But you say, "What can I give to God?" First, yourself - live your life to please Him. Second, your time - take time to worship and serve Him. Third, your possessions - some things you own can be used by God or you can share with Him the money you have. With such sacrifices God is well pleased.

MAY 24　　JUDGES 14:1-9

One day I was canoeing down a quiet, peaceful river, when all of a sudden I heard a bang, followed by a long scraping sound. Underneath the water was a huge rock. Being just below the surface, I hadn't seen it. Yet the damage was done.

Samson saw a beautiful girl whom he wanted as his wife. The problem was, she was a Philistine. God forebade the marriage of Israelites to other peoples. He realized the difference in belief and culture would cause trouble. A quick reading of the Old Testament shows that whenever Israel went after foreign wives they soon forgot their God and worshipped the gods of the foreigners. The New Testament also teaches that we as Christians should only marry other Christians (2 Corinthians 6:14).

MAY 25　　JUDGES 14:10-20

The passage shows to us the completely undisciplined character of Samson. First, he rejects the advice of his parents and proceeds to marry this Philistine girl. Then during the wedding feast he sets forth a riddle that no one could know. He uses it as a means of gaining wealth from them. Then when the riddle is found out, in anger and revenge he goes to another

Philistine city, kills 30 men, using their clothes to pay off his debt. Then, forsaking his wife, he returns home. Samson had the same attitude of many today. "I alone am important; I will do what I want, when I want." The Lord wants us to be concerned, disciplined people.

MAY 26   JUDGES 15:1-8

Once when I was young, I planted some green bean seeds. It was thrilling to watch them grow. Finally, little green beans began to appear. I expected them. I would have been surprised if an ear of corn or a pumpkin had appeared on the plant. It is an accepted principle that whatever seed you plant that's the type of plant that will grow. It's also true in other areas. The type of life I live today will determine what will happen to me in the future.

Samson's wife tried to save her life by cheating Samson rather than trusting in him to protect her. This began a series of events that ended in her death. What type of life are you living today?

MAY 27   JUDGES 15:9-20

Have you ever been mad at someone so you did something against them? They in turn did something to pay you back, and so on it goes. This is what Samson got himself into. Revenge seeks further revenge until one or the other is destroyed. For Samson it led to his death. But is this the Christian way to handle things? Christ wants me to forgive others, not to pay them back. I am to give up my rights to other people. By doing this I live my life centered around others and not around myself. This is the attitude displayed by Christ when He died on the cross. He died for me, not for Himself. Let us imitate Him.

MAY 28   JUDGES 16:1-9

The Bible never tries to hide anything about the men whom God uses for His purposes. Many of the great men of the Old Testament had weaknesses which God exposes in His Book. Samson was unable to control his emotional passion for love. As we look at Samson's three loves, recorded for us, we discover each one got him in trouble, the final one led to his death. It seems that in each of us Satan finds a weak spot on which he works in his attempt to make us useless for God. Are you living totally for Christ, or are there areas in your life that are not yet turned over to Him?

MAY 29   JUDGES 16:10-17

In this passage we see an example of how sin blinds. How a man like Samson could continually be tested as to what he said was the source of his power, and then go on in the end to actually reveal the true source of that power, is beyond reason. Yet, this is characteristic of sin. We become so taken up with the desire for the pleasure of the present that we don't think about the results of our sin. Samson's failure to think cost him his life. We see the need here of reading the Bible and praying every day. By keeping our minds on Christ we can avoid many of the pitfalls of sin.

MAY 30   JUDGES 16:18-22

"...he did not know that the Lord had departed from him" (verse 20).

Samson had been called by God, before his birth, to deliver his people. He was set aside by God as a Nazarite. He was never to cut his hair, drink strong wine, or touch a dead body. With his hair cut, Samson's vow before the Lord was broken. The man who could have been so much for the Lord now stood forsaken by Him. Is it not true that the only way a person can find purpose and satisfaction in life is in a personal relationship with God? This we can have by placing our faith in Jesus Christ. Where are you today? Forsaken by God, or a child of God?

MAY 31   JUDGES 16:23-31

Isn't our God a great God? There is none in the universe who can be compared in any way with Him. Read Isaiah 40:18-31. It is God who is in control of the affairs of man. Man does not make his own history. God puts in power those He wants and removes others. God uses nations like the Midianites and the Philistines to punish His people when they sin. He uses many types of people, like Gideon and Samson, to deliver His people when they call on Him. What a tremendous God we have! Let us worship, obey and serve Him.

JUNE 1   JOB 1:1-13

God describes Job:"upright...one that feareth God and turneth away from evil" (verse 8). Satan was not impressed. He thought Job would change if God's "hedge" was removed (verse 11). What was this hedge? (Read verses 2, 3, and 10.) Job had everything, and Satan thought that he would quickly turn from God if the security of his family and possessions was removed. Maybe you have a "hedge" around you just now. Everything is going your way. You have done well in school. You have a happy circle of friends. Your parents have agreed to allow you to go to summer camp. What if these things were removed? Do you try to please God because things are going your way, or because He is God, and God knows best?

JUNE 2   JOB 1:14-22

Wow! Talk about "bad news"! Remember that "hedge" in yesterday's reading? It is gone! Satan has destroyed Job's hundreds of animals, and all the servants that looked after them. He is no longer a man of great possessions. And, as if this were not enough, his ten children are dead - killed in a wind storm that crumbled their house! News of these terrible events comes quickly to Job, and suddenly he finds himself standing all alone. He feels naked. Notice his reaction (verses 20-22). Especially notice that Satan was wrong about Job. Compare verse 11 with verse 22. How do you react toward God when even one important thing or person in your life is removed? Think carefully about verses 20-22, remembering Job's great losses.

JUNE 3   JOB 2:1-13

Poor Job. Satan is not finished with him yet. On top of all he has lost, we find him covered from head to foot with painful boils, sitting in ashes, scraping himself with a broken dish (verses 7-8). His own wife speaks against his brave attitude (verse 9). Job's sorrow is very deep, and his so-called friends watch him in silence (verse 13). Some people know what physical suffering is. Few of us will ever suffer what Job did in addition to his great sorrow of heart. Yet how we complain! Regardless of how difficult things become, complaining against God is wrong. It means I do not trust Him to do what is best. Satan's third effort had failed. Job did not sin with his lips (verse 10).

JUNE 4   JOB 42:1-17

God has been speaking to Job and today's verses contain Job's answer. Notice what he says in verse 2. Do you know what this means? Think of it this way. Often we make plans and decide in our minds how they will work out. Our thoughts contain our plans or purposes. However, many things can interfere with our plans, leaving us terribly disappointed. Things like people and circumstances can change everything. God's plans are not like that. This verse says that God's thoughts cannot be stopped. If God purposes in His mind to do something for you, nothing that another person does or says, no circumstance, can hold back His purpose. Do you believe that? Job did. Read Isaiah 14:24 and 27.

JUNE 5   PSALM 90:1-9

Do you have any "secret sins"? Moses did, and he knew that his people did (verse 8). Is there a lie that no one knows about? Are your thoughts always good? Are they clean? What about school? Have you ever cheated on a test, or in your homework? There may be other things that make you feel badly, but you have kept them secret. You would probably feel very embarrassed and ashamed if you thought anyone knew. Sometimes we forget that our "secrets" are known by God. We talk to Him about everything else but carefully avoid mention of these things. God knows us well. Read Psalm 139:1-6. Let us not imagine that any sin goes unseen by Him.

JUNE 6   PSALM 90:10-17

The Israelites who left Egypt with Moses were very stubborn and rebellious. God disciplined their disobedience in the wilderness again and again. Read Numbers 14:26-35. What terrible news! They were told that those twenty years and older were doomed to die in the wilderness before the Promised Land was reached. Only their children would enter the land. Moses wrote the sad words in today's verses after receiving this news from God. Notice his request in verses 12 and 17. Even though he knew their doom, Moses was concerned about what they did with the time left to them. Sometimes we do not spend our time wisely. Much of it is wasted. We cannot expect God to bless our efforts if we waste His time.

JUNE 7   PSALM 91:1-16

This is a Psalm about security. Do you remember how

you felt on your first day at camp when all the faces were strange and you did not know your way around? It was not a very secure feeling. But remember how it was after only a few days? You had a good circle of friends, a great counsellor, and everything had become familiar. You felt happy. You began to feel as though you had been there for weeks. You were feeling secure. Psalm 91 talks about the person who has made God his "habitation", his living place (verse 9). The constant awareness of God's presence gives this person

security in every situation. He knows God is with Him.
Read the Psalm again.

JUNE 8   PSALM 92:1-15

Sometimes the circumstances of our lives seem unfair.
We try to please God and do what is right, and yet at times,
things seem to go better for our friends who do not care about
God. Verse 7 talks about this and says it will not always be
so. God's thoughts are very deep (verse 5). Try to remember
that He knows a great deal more than you. He sees the end
from the beginning, and we are seeing only the present when
we begin to feel that God is unfair with us. Notice the decla-
ration in the last verse. God is upright. There is no unrighteousness in Him. Although God's ways with us may not
always seem fair, they are always right.

JUNE 9   PSALM 93:1-5

A testimony is what a person says. Verse 5 declares that
God's "testimonies are very sure." In other words, whatever
God says is sure. You can count on it! One of the things He
has said is in verse 1. "The Lord reigneth." Sometimes it
looks as if God has lost control, doesn't it? A few years ago,
some people began to advertise that God was dead. They did
not recognize any evidence of His control. Sometimes we may
go through very difficult situations when everything seems
out of control. Accidents, sickness, and hurts of all kinds may
be part of our circumstances. In such a time, learn to count on
what God has said. "The Lord reigneth." God IS in control.

JUNE 10   1 PETER 1:1-12

Not may years after Christ was crucified, the Christians
were cruelly persecuted and forced to flee to many parts of
the world. Peter writes to these scattered believers. He
expresses thankfulness to God for raising Jesus Christ from
the dead. The Christian's hope is in a *living* Saviour. He
speaks of the certainty of the Christian's inheritance in heav-
en, and the protecting power of God. He sympathizes with
their grief in the awful trials of persecution and says the
results will be proof of their faith in the unseen Christ. Then

he reminds them that the understanding of their salvation in Jesus Christ is something that neither the prophets nor the angels possessed. Can you find these thoughts in today's verses?

JUNE 11   1 PETER 1:13-21

Peter's letter to the scattered believers continues. He concentrates on two important parts of Christian living - hope and obedience. He encourages them to keep central in their minds their sure *hope* of the return of Jesus Christ. Then he reminds them of how they used to behave before they knew God as their Father. He tells them that the old behaviour ought to change. They are to live now in *obedience* to a holy God, remembering that their lives have been saved by the death and resurrection of Jesus Christ, not by any price they themselves have paid. Never forget that Jesus Christ will return. In light of this *hope*, let us behave in *obedience* to the One whose blood was shed for us.

JUNE 12   1 PETER 1:22-25

Peter declares that God's Word will never be destroyed (verses 23-25). The reason for this fact is clear. What God says is *true*, and truth does not die. We can do many things with the truth. We can ignore it, mock it, rebel against it, twist it, hide it, or even deny it, but we cannot destroy it. Truth remains. Peter says that these people have "purified their souls in *obedience* to the truth" (verse 22). They have chosen to obey God's Word and one evidence of their obedience is their sincere love for each other (verses 22). John 13:35

I'm ok!

TRUTH

says, "By this shall all men know that ye are my disciples, if ye have love one to another." What are you doing with God's truth?

JUNE 13   1 PETER 2:1-10

Healthy babies have good appetites. Have you ever seen a hungry baby? He loses interest in his toys, and neither your lullabies nor any amount of cuddling will soothe and quiet him. He has one desire that no distraction can satisfy. He wants his milk! Peter says that the Christian's desire for God's Word ought to be like this (verse 2). We should hunger for it. How easily we are distracted from reading the Bible each day! We make time for many other less important things and come to the end of the day with the excuse that we have not had time to read. A hungry baby cannot be distracted, and a baby with a poor appetite is a sick baby. How is your appetite for God's Word?

JUNE 14   1 PETER 2:11-17

Wow! Today's verses are important! Did you know that your behaviour could cause an enemy of Jesus Christ to glorify God (verse 12)? Your behaviour can even cause a foolish person to be quiet (verse 15)! The behaviour of a Christian is what people see, and often it is the only thing to do with God that they will watch. Stay away from every desire that conflicts with your spiritual life (verse 11). This may be as obvious as eating too much, or not getting enough sleep. Obey the authorities over you (verses 13-14) - this includes our city laws, your school rules, regulations at camp, the expectations of your parents. These things seem simple, but they are noticed - first by God Himself, then by people around us. Your behaviour counts!

JUNE 15   1 PETER 2:18-25

How would you feel if someone took the blame and punishment for something you had done wrong? Suppose the punishment was very severe and the person suffered great pain without a word about how unfair it was. Would you not hurt deeply for him? Would you feel differently if this person were suffering for something he himself had done? Peter speaks frequently about suffering in his letters to the persecuted believers. Verses 18-20 describe two kinds of suffering. Notice that one is particularly "acceptable with God" (verse 20), and describe it. Christ suffered this way. Read the rest of the passage carefully and consider His attitude. The injustices you may suffer will never be as great as those He went through. How does your attitude compare with His?

JUNE 16   1 PETER 3:1-6

Most of us are concerned about how we look. We are happy when someone admires our hair or something we are wearing. We want to dress in popular fashions and are anxious for approval, especially from our friends. This is good, unless it becomes more important to us than it should. Read again verses 3 and 4. In God's eyes, your inward appearance is of greater value than your outward appearance. In other words, He would have you more concerned with the part of you which will live forever than with that part which must one day die and be buried. God places more value on the development of a meek and quiet spirit than on buying new clothes. Which truly is more important to you?

JUNE 17   1 PETER 3:7-12

There is great power in the tongue which needs careful control. Look at verse 10. Your tongue is capable of evil: unkind words, gossip, exaggeration, complaining, lies, destructive criticism, dirty language, deception, swearing, breaking of confidences - can you

add to the list? Now read thoughtfully James 3:3-12. We have a serious problem. The tongue can hurt and damage almost without our knowing it. Did you know that? There exists a species of elephant in Africa which man has never been able to tame. They are vicious and dangerous. James says, "the tongue can no man

tame" (verse 8). It is like this African elephant. David must
have known its awful power, and he had the only answer. Read
Psalm 141.3. God must control my words.

JUNE 18   1 PETER 3:13-22

Peter never forgets that he is writing to people who
suffer severe persecution because of their Christianity. He
continually encourages them with the reminder of Christ's
suffering, and in the midst of this is verse 15. The Christian
has a hope that is the possession only of God's children. How
prepared are you to explain to another the reason for your
hope in God - your relationship with Him because of Jesus
Christ? If your life impresses people, they may one day ask
you what makes you different. Would that question frighten
you or could you answer well? The early Christians had
reason to be afraid for their lives, yet Peter said, "Be ready!"
God says, "Be ready always to give an answer."

JUNE 19   1 PETER 4:1-6

Your mind is an important part of you. It affects everything about you - your actions, words, feelings, and attitudes.
Peter mentions the mind in verse 1, and it is as if he were
saying, "Get this through your head, Christian. You will
suffer." Apparently some believers were complaining bit-
terly, saying something like this, "I should not have to suffer.
I am a Christian. I belong to God!" Peter explains that people
disliked them because they refused to participate in sin.
Christ suffered as a man because, being without sin, He was
different. As you mingle with people who do not belong to
God, you too will be different - and you will suffer. God
knows. Do not think it strange. Read verses 12 and 13.

JUNE 20   1 PETER 4:7-11

Can you remember awakening on a morning close to the
end of your summer holidays and realizing that you had only
a few days left? You wanted to make the most of every
minute and not waste any time. I think this is how Peter must
have been feeling when he wrote these verses. With the
return of Jesus Christ, opportunity to bring Him glory in this
world will end, and Peter did not know how soon that would

be. He encourages these Christians to make the best of every minute. Think clearly and pray (verse 7). Love each other sincerely (verse 8). Be hospitable to your friends without complaining (verse 9). Use your talents well because they are God's gifts (verses 10 and 11). The end of all things will come!

JUNE 21   1 PETER 4:12-19

Has anyone ever told you to mind your own business? You may have resented it and felt angry at their rudeness to you. Yet the person may have had good reason for the comment. If you read God's Word carefully, you will find that you do not like everything it says. But this does not change the truth of it. Read verse 15. If you must be punished for being "a busybody in other men's matters," you dishonour God as does a murderer or a thief. A 'busybody' gossips, is nosey, and speaks out of turn when he ought to be silent. These things seem less important to us than murder or stealing, but God lists them together. Learn to mind your own business!

JUNE 22   1 PETER 5:1-7

Are you a leader or a follower? Probably you are both. If your mother leaves you in charge of your younger brothers and sisters, you are a leader. You must make the decisions and give directions to the others. However, there are many situations at your age where you are a follower, the person taking instructions from another. Peter speaks to leaders and followers. Both should dress alike - clothed with *humility* (verse 5). Whether you are leading others or following a leader, do not act as if you 'know it all'. That is pride, and God resists proud people (verse 5). He wants you to come to Him with every problem (verse 7). How sad if He must resist you when you come! Ask God now to help you learn humility.

JUNE 23   1 PETER 5:8-14

Have you ever watched a lion? He plants his huge paws in silence, like a cat, and you do not hear him walking. When he roars, it is usually because he is hungry and unable to find food. Peter's description of Satan in verse 8 is very accurate.

The Devil creeps silently into your path and you do not hear his approach. His hunger is to see people sin against God, and he seeks you as a hungry lion seeks for food. He walks about looking for opportunities to satisfy this evil desire. Satan is still very much alive today, and Peter tells the Christians to *resist* him. The best way you can resist the devil is to *obey* God. Read James 4:7.

JUNE 24   2 PETER 1:1-8

Have you ever felt that your life was empty and not very worthwhile? Even a person who *knows* God through Jesus Christ can feel this way about himself, and it can, in fact, be true. Three times in these verses Peter mentions our *knowledge* of Jesus Christ. Through it we can experience grace and peace (verse 2), all that we need to live the kind of life intended by God (verse 3), and the fulfillment of His great promises to make us like Himself (verse 4). But Peter says in verse 8 that if our lives are to count, we must want to have in us those things listed in verses 5, 6 and 7.

JUNE 25   2 PETER 1:9-15

How good is your memory? Just as our bodies need exercise to keep physically fit, so our memories must be exercised to function well. Can you remember what you read in God's Word yesterday? How about last week? Peter knew that these Christians needed to be reminded of things they had already heard (verses 12 and 13). He wanted these truths planted deeply in their minds so that after he was dead they would never forget them (verses 14 and 15). Look at verse

9. Peter is talking about a "blind" Christian. This person does not exercise his memory about God's truth, with the result that he cannot see how God wants him to live. He even forgets that his sins have been forgiven! It is important to *remember* what God says.

JUNE 26   2 PETER 1:16-21

One day you may be asked to testify in a court of law. The judge will listen only to what you actually saw or heard. Your *opinion* of the case will not be considered. He will want the *facts*. The men that God used to write the Scriptures testified this way. Notice that Peter speaks of what they had seen (verse 16), and what they had heard (verses 17 and 18). What they wrote down afterwards was a "sure word" (verse 19). We can count on its truth! Just as the prophets spoke by the direction of the Holy Spirit, so these men wrote under His direction (verse 21). Do not ever think that the Scriptures contain simply the opinions of men. The Bible is God's Word, and it comes to us with certainty from Himself.

JUNE 27   2 PETER 2:1-11

Have you ever passed a swimming test? If so, you probably had a good teacher. Sometimes an examiner does not pass a swimmer because the swimmer has been taught incorrectly. You would feel badly if you performed your skills for the examiner exactly as your teacher had taught, only to find that they were wrong. Peter refers to people who teach others about God and he calls some of them "false teachers" (verse 1). These persons do not teach the truth about God, and Peter says that many people will believe what they say (verses 1 and 2). How sad for those people when God examines their beliefs and finds them incorrect. The Bible is true. Any teaching that disagrees with what the Bible says is false.

JUNE 28   2 PETER 2:12-22

God will deal severely with false teachers. They not only lose out themselves, but they are responsible for misleading others. They have "forsaken the right way" (verse 15). May that never be said of you. God says in verse 21 that it would be better for such a person never to have known the truth! Perhaps you have been taught the truth about God as long as you can remember. It will not always be so. The world is full of false teachers who will try to destroy your faith. There may be one in your own home. There are surely some in your school. They can sometimes make their ideas seem very right. Do not be deceived. Remember - what the Bible says is true.

JUNE 29   2 PETER 3:1-10

When we are young, we tend to think that things will go on for ever as they always have. We somehow ignore the idea of change, especially if we find ourselves in happy circumstances. If a man loses his job through sudden illness or accident, and the family is faced with long months of poverty, it is a great shock to everyone. Read verses 3 and 4 again. Most people are so accustomed to the world as it is, that the changes which must occur with the second coming of Jesus Christ are ignored. Christ's return will be a great shock to them, but it should be no surprise to the Christian. We believe God!

JUNE 30   2 PETER 3:11-18

BLAMELESS! That is quite a word. You will find it in verse 14. It means without blame. It means not guilty of sin. Peter speaks to the Christians who look for Christ's return, and says that He should find them blameless when He comes. In other words, the person who expects Christ to come again will not ignore sin. My sins must be confessed to God; and if I am to be blameless, I must receive His forgiveness. You see, Christ took the blame for my sins on the cross. By His death, my guilt is removed, as long as I go to Him for forgiveness. Jesus Christ cannot tolerate sin. See that He finds you blameless when He comes.

JULY 1   1 SAMUEL 1:1-8

Today we begin a new book. 1 Samuel is fascinating because we can see God working in people's lives. Before the end of this month we will read about Samuel's beginnings and growth as a man of God. Samuel was greatly respected by the Jews. Only Moses was thought to be more important.

We will watch as the people beg for a king to rule them because they did not like being different from the people around them. Before this month is over we will see Israel's first king crowned and then we will follow him as he begins his reign.

In today's passage we are introduced to Samuel's family. Watch carefully as this family grows and influences other people.

JULY 2   1 SAMUEL 1:9-18

Hannah is extremely sad. Peninnah is constantly annoying her because she is unable to have children. Finally Hannah becomes so discouraged that she cries and refuses to eat. Elkanah fails to comfort her. When she gets to the temple, she pours out her soul to the Lord. As a Christian that should be your *first* action. Turn your problems over to Him and He will help you solve them.

Eli made a mistake that most of us make. He thought the worst of Hannah. She looked as though she was drunk but he should have been sure of his facts before he accused her. I think Eli learned his lesson. Have you?

JULY 3   1 SAMUEL 1:19-28

It must have been very difficult for Hannah to take her much loved son to the temple and give him to the Lord. However, if God asks us to sacrifice for Him, He will replace the loss with something better. In 1 Samuel 2:21 we learn that Hannah was given five more children. God asks all of us to make sacrifices. Some people lose their friends when they begin to live the Christian life but God gives them new and better friends. All of us have to sacrifice some of our spare time activities in order to spend time with God in His Word, but look at the promises God makes to those who do so... Joshua 1:8; Psalm 1:2,3. We can be sure that God will richly repay us for any sacrifice we make for Him.

JULY 4   1 SAMUEL 2:1-11

Frequently in the Bible God is called a Rock. In Psalm 31:3, David calls God "my Rock and my Fortress." David had been through many dangerous times and he had discovered that God could give better security and protection than anyone else. In verse 2 we find that Hannah had also learned that lesson. Those who think that they can run their own life will soon discover that they need God's help. List the things that could happen to the proud according to this passage. Now list the things that God will do for His people. Are you trusting in the Rock?

JULY 5   1 SAMUEL 2:12-26

When Eli lived the people depended on the priests to show them what God was like. The priests taught them about God and offered sacrifices to Him for them. We read here that Eli's sons were not followers of God. They were evil men who showed the people a wrong picture of God.

Just as Eli's sons were poor pictures of God, so are many people who call themselves Christians. There are a lot of people today who do not go to a church or read a Bible. YOU are the only picture they see of God. Is it a clear picture?

JULY 6   1 SAMUEL 2:27-36

God was not pleased with Eli and punished him because he did not discipline his sons. Many of us are guilty of a mistake that is worse than Eli's. We know of sin in our own life but we ignore it. God reminds Eli of the marvellous things that He had done for Eli and the Israelites but tells him that he is spoiling it because he is allowing his sons to sin. God has given us many good gifts like allowing us to walk with Him every day and talk to Him at any time. But, if we do not confess our sin and ask God's help to not sin again, then this beautiful relationship is spoiled and we cannot fully enjoy His gifts.

JULY 7   1 SAMUEL 3:1-10

Please notice that Samuel was ministering unto the Lord. What he probably was doing was cleaning the temple, polishing the candlesticks, running the errands, filling the lampstand with oil. Samuel was Eli's servant and anything that Eli wanted him to do Samuel did. Verse 5 shows how quickly he obeyed even in the middle of the night. Samuel was a willing worker because he knew he was actually serving God. 1 Corinthians 10:31b says to do everything to God's glory. If your parents tell you to do something, then do it to God's glory. If your teachers give you something to do, then do it for the Lord.

JULY 8   1 SAMUEL 3:11-21

Yesterday Samuel was working for God's glory. Sometimes God gives us a job that we do not want. Perhaps like the ones yesterday, it is too humble or it takes too long or it is too dangerous. However, if we do not carry out the responsibilities that God has given us now, He will not trust us with anything more. Samuel did not like the first message that he was told to deliver. It was a very unpleasant message that would hurt his friend, Eli, so Samuel wanted to hide the message from him. Verse 18 says, "Samuel told him everything, and hid nothing from him." Because Samuel carried out his duty he "grew, and the Lord was with him."

JULY 9   1 SAMUEL 4:1-11

The "ark of the covenant of the Lord" was a box that God told Moses to build to symbolize His presence among the people of Israel. In verse 3, the elders of Israel made the mistake of believing that the symbol would save them from their enemies, instead of the actual presence of God. Many times we do the same thing. We can become so busy doing Christian things that we forget about God. We can go to church without worshipping God. We can read our Bibles out of habit without letting God speak to us. We can even pray without really speaking to God. These things are good only if they are genuine. If they are not done with meaning, they are worthless.

JULY 10   1 SAMUEL 4:12-22

Remember the sad news Samuel told Eli in chapter 2? God had said that He would judge Eli. Here is the punishment. Eli's two sons have been killed and the messenger just blurts it out to Eli. What a shock to that old man! But the messenger didn't stop there. "The ark has been taken by the enemy." That was too much for Eli and he fell back off his seat and broke his neck. His family was gone and the symbol of God was removed. He must have been very sad to see his life just about wasted. The things he was supposed to do were not done, or they were done wrong. Now is the time for you to correct your mistakes. Ask God to show you what is displeasing to Him and then ask Him to help you change before it is too late.

JULY 11   1 SAMUEL 5:1-12

Last week we learned that God is the strongest Rock that anyone can trust in. The poor Philistines didn't know that. They had heard many things about the God of the Israelites (1 Samuel 4:8) and they knew He was powerful but they preferred to trust their idol, Dagon. Isn't it exciting that God even made Dagon bow down to Him? However, it wasn't until they had gone through several disasters that they realized they must give God His proper place and send the symbol of His presence back to Israel. Let us make sure that we give God His proper place so we don't have to learn the hard way.

JULY 12   1 SAMUEL 6:1-9

The Philistines' situation was very much like that of the Egyptians (Exodus 7-12). Both nations refused to obey God. He wanted the Egyptians to let His people go and He wanted the Philistines to let His ark go. Remember the plagues the Egyptians suffered? The Philistines didn't learn. If they had they would have been saved a lot of trouble. We often cause ourselves unnecessary trouble because we do not learn from our past mistakes and from those of the Bible characters. We just keep on doing the same thing again and again. Take note of all the mistakes and see if you can avoid them in your life.

JULY 13   1 SAMUEL 6:10-21

Who is able to stand before this Holy Lord God? When
you think of God, do you picture a kind old man with white
hair and a beard smiling down on the earth? These verses
should destroy that picture. God is *holy!* He has set down
rules that cannot be broken. When He speaks we should
obey. The men at Bethshemesh should have known better
than to touch the ark, let alone look inside it. The Books of
Exodus and Leviticus have many passages that describe in
detail how the ark was to be handled. Only a certain group of
the Levites could carry it and no one else was to touch it. The
men of Bethshemesh did not respect God's law. We can be
sure of punishment if we disobey His commands.

JULY 14   1 SAMUEL 7:1-8

Samuel shows that he has the authority of God as he tells
the people to turn from their idols back to God. Samuel tells
them to return to the Lord with *all* their heart. They were
being half-hearted followers of God. Their love and service
was divided between God and their idols, Baalim and Ashta-
roth. Do you serve the Lord only? Jesus said that the first
commandment was to "love the Lord thy God with all thy
heart, with all thy soul, and with all thy mind" (Matthew
22:37). That's what it means to serve the Lord whole-heart-
edly.

JULY 15   1 SAMUEL 7:9-17

Samuel put that stone in place and called it Ebenezer to
remind the Israelites that God had helped them. You ought to
have an Ebenezer. Think back in your life to a point where
God helped you. It probably won't be as exciting as a really
wild thunderstorm but that is not important. As you continue
to grow in your Christian life and you see God do things in
your life, your Ebenezer will change. You may get discouraged and wonder if God really does exist or help in your life
and then you can think of your Ebenezer and thank the Lord.

JULY 16   1 SAMUEL 8:1-9

We have learned something of God's power so far this
month. He gave Hannah a child and defeated the Philistines.

The Bible is just full of evidence of His power. Wasn't the nation of Israel privileged to have such a mighty God as their king! He could have made them the greatest and most wonderful nation this world has ever known if they had allowed Him to rule but they were not satisfied with God as king.

You are just as fortunate as Israel because God wants to be your king. He can do as much in your life as in Israel if you will let Him rule.

JULY 17   1 SAMUEL 8:10-22

Israel wanted a king so that they would be just like the nations around them but they didn't look closely to see what effect a king would have on them. Since kings are powerful and like to live in luxury, he was going to take the best of everything for himself; the best vineyards, the best fields, the best servants, the best flocks and cattle and the best young men. The people would have to give up all that and pay taxes as well.

Sometimes we get mad at God because He does not give us what we want. We forget that God is all-wise and knows far better than we do what is best for us. Sometimes He allows us to have what we ask for in order to teach us some lessons and bring us closer to Himself.

JULY 18   1 SAMUEL 9:1-14

Saul is described in verse 2 as being a handsome man, more handsome than all the children of Israel. He was also taller than anyone else. Every place Saul went all the people would turn to get a sight of such a good-looking man. He was also obedient because he took a lot of time to find his father's donkeys. Are these enough good points to make him king? Look back to 1 Samuel 3:19. Samuel grew and the Lord was with him. That is a much better way to be effective. Don't get caught looking at the *outside* appearance of people. It is what is *inside* that really matters. Remember - God looks at the heart.

JULY 19   1 SAMUEL 9:15-27

God used some donkeys to bring Saul a long way to meet with Samuel. God had told Samuel that Saul was coming and to expect him. I'm sure that Saul was not very thrilled when he left his father's house to look for the donkeys. Little did he know that God was working in his life. God works in similar ways today. If you have given control of your life to Him, then everything that happens to you is directed by God. Are you learning from those situations? Maybe God is preparing you to be a great man or woman for Him.

JULY 20   1 SAMUEL 10:1-8

The events that were to happen to Saul were indications that God was choosing him especially to do a job for Him. God's prophets would recognize those signs immediately and welcome him as one of them. God gives gifts to His people today as well. Read 1 Corinthians 12. Some of you teens ought to look at your life to see which of those gifts you have. Ask God to help you develop them.

Watch and see if Saul does what he was told to do.

JULY 21   1 SAMUEL 10:9-16

This was a good beginning for Saul. "The spirit of God came upon him." This means that at that point he was very close to God. God was speaking to him and through him to others. He was one of the prophets or men of God. We read earlier that he was the people's choice because of his outward appearance. His qualifications weren't very good then but now he has God's help. Saul did a good job when he obeyed God and stayed close to Him. When he disobeyed and tried to reign by himself, things were disastrous.

JULY 22   1 SAMUEL 10:17-27

This is a sad passage. At the coronation of the king, the first in Israel, Samuel gives a warning. "You have rejected God," he says. These people could recall so many, many times that God had acted on their behalf. All the memories they had of God were of good things He had done for them. One drawback was that He had given them commands. They were a little too strict. So they broke them which messed up their lives. They got so far away from Him that He gave in to their wishes and gave them a king. Are you breaking God's laws?

JULY 23   1 SAMUEL 11:1-15

The phrase, "and the Spirit of God came upon Saul" is very important. This is the second time we have come across it. The first time was soon after he had found out that God was going to make him king of the Israelites. Now a group of Israelites were about to be tortured by the Ammonites and "the Spirit of God came upon Saul" and enabled him to raise over 300,000 men to go down and fight the Ammonites. Saul's men defeated the enemy and saved their people. This time Saul gives the glory to God where it belongs.

JULY 24   1 SAMUEL 12:1-5

Samuel has grown old. Old people are usually ignored or tolerated rather than loved and respected. Samuel had spent almost all his life serving the people of Israel for the Lord. Here he calls the people together to see if he has done anything to make them angry or annoyed. They all had to admit he had been honest and fair. What a tribute to a man who had lived for God all those years! Even with those qualifications the people ignored his urgings and rejected God.

JULY 25   1 SAMUEL 12:6-15

Saul is now the King of Israel but Samuel reminds the people that God still requires them to obey His law. There is no other choice for the person who says he is a follower of God. These people chose a human king and forgot God. As a Christian you have chosen the KING OF KINGS as your king. Verse 14 tells us how this should affect you: "serve Him, obey Him, and do not rebel against His commandments." Does that describe how you treat your king?

JULY 26   1 SAMUEL 12:16-25

Here is another warning from Samuel to keep the commands of the Lord. This time he asked the Lord to give his words more authority by a supernatural sign. God did not do

this to show Samuel's power but to remind the Israelites of His power. Can you think of other times He showed His power? It worked. The people realized their sin and said that they would always follow God's commands.

Samuel gives very good advice to the people in verse 21. For us "vain things" are things like sports, education, success, money, etc. These things will not be of any use to us in God's eyes. Jesus said, "Seek ye *first* the kingdom of God..." (Matthew 6:33).

JULY 27   1 SAMUEL 13:1-10

A few days ago we read that Samuel had told Saul to wait seven days for him to come down and make sacrifices. As God's representative he was supposed to offer the sacrifices. This was Saul's first major mistake as king - he disobeyed God. His position as king went to his head and he forgot that it was God who won the first battle. Does that happen to you? Things are going well with God's help and you begin living without His help which only causes problems. The problem really is *DISOBEDIENCE*.

JULY 28   1 SAMUEL 13:11-23

Saul began to make excuses. Remember when your counsellor caught you where you were out of bounds? You began to make excuses and blame your buddy. Saul knew he had been wrong but he had been afraid. The enemy was coming and his men were poor fighters so he was afraid. He forgot that God would protect His own people. He had seen God work before but he seems to have forgotten. Saul was not a very strong character. He tried to put the blame on Samuel for being late and the enemy for being so close. He simply didn't trust God. Do you trust God for *all* the details in your life?

JULY 29   1 SAMUEL 14:1-18

Jonathan was just a young man but he knew that God could do anything. He also had learned that God uses people to show what He wants you to do. Here it was the words the Philistines used to shout at Jonathan. As soon as he heard them he knew that God would help him win. Twenty men were killed that day by Jonathan and his friend and they started the battle.

Have you ever thought of asking God to help you accomplish something for Him? That's the key: remember - *for Him*. Paul said, "I can do *all* things through Christ who strengthens me" (Philippians 4:13).

JULY 30   1 SAMUEL 14:19-35

Saul had made an oath to God which was something that could not be broken. It appears that one reason he did it is that he was the king. It was HE that was to be avenged. The people of God were to kill the Philistines for SAUL'S sake. It should have been for GOD's sake. It wasn't even a good oath because food gives strength to fight better. Jonathan ate some food and a little later many people began eating some meat that wasn't prepared according to God's law. If Saul hadn't made that oath, the people would have eaten properly and not sinned.

WHAT we say and WHY we say it are important to God. Listen carefully to yourself today when you talk.

JULY 31   1 SAMUEL 14:36-46

When God didn't answer Saul, he knew that there was sin among the people. It was in Jonathan, the one who had killed 20 men and started the battle with God's help. The Bible says that the people rescued Jonathan. The oath could not be broken but it could be satisfied by the offering of a sacrifice or the paying of a certain amount of money. Jonathan would have been very grateful to them for rescuing him from death. Remember that Jesus did the same thing for us except the cost was much higher - His life. Be grateful.

AUGUST 1   1 SAMUEL 15:1-9

I wish I were a king or queen - then I wouldn't have to obey anybody. Wrong. God requires obedience from *all*. King Saul was ordered by God to completely wipe out the Amalekite people. They had defied God for the last time. Off went Saul with his army, fought the Amalekites and defeated them. That's a good start. But look at verse 9. Saul saved their king, the best of their sheep and cattle, and brought them all back with him. By doing this he deliberately disobeyed God, and that can only bring sorrow.

AUGUST 2   1 SAMUEL 15:10-23

God is never pleased when we disobey Him, and it makes no difference whether we are kings or campers. God sent Samuel to tell King Saul this. When Samuel arrived

moo!

Saul said, "I have done everything God asked!" "That's odd," said Samuel, "then what is all the racket I hear...bleating of sheep and mooing of cows?" "Oh that!" said Saul, "just the odd souvenir the people brought back. It's to give to the Lord, of course." Now he blamed the people. Samuel had serious words for Saul; words from God. Said Samuel, "God sent you on a special job for Him, and you chose to disobey. Now hear this. God wants obedience, not gifts. Because of your sin God has rejected you as king." Saul paid a high price for disobedience. So must we all.

AUGUST 3   1 SAMUEL 15:24-35

King Saul confessed that he had disobeyed God but said it was because he was afraid of the people. Afraid? How? Of not pleasing them. This is true of us. We do something we *know* is wrong just to please our friends, not God. Beware of pleasing *anyone* but God. Samuel went home very upset about Saul's actions and hoping things would change. But God knew Saul's thoughts for He saw Saul's heart just as He sees ours. He knows not only what we do, but what we *intend* to do (Hebrews 4:12). Think about that for a while.

AUGUST 4   1 SAMUEL 16:1-5

Everyone has difficulties and this includes the Christian. The difference is the Christian knows Who is in charge. So it was with Samuel. He was saddened that Saul was rejected, but he accepted God's judgment. Now God had a man in mind to replace Saul and he asked Samuel to go and anoint him. (This was done by pouring oil on the chosen person's head.) In verse 4 we find Samuel "did what the Lord said" (A.V.). That's obedience.

AUGUST 5   1 SAMUEL 16:6-13

Samuel was sent to a man named Jesse, as God's choice was one of Jesse's eight sons. Beginning at the eldest they came in to meet Samuel. The first was tall and handsome and Samuel almost jumped to his feet to anoint him. "Surely he *must* be the one!" he thought. But the Lord said, "Hold it, Samuel! You are looking on the outside, but I can see the heart." Like Samuel we judge people by their appearance, but God knows what we *really* are. Seven sons met Samuel and none was chosen. Then Jesse said there was one more - just a lad - minding the sheep. "Bring him in," said Samuel. As he entered the Lord said to Samuel, "Rise up! Anoint him!'' David, the youngest, the least important - but *right* in God's sight.

AUGUST 6   1 SAMUEL 16:14-23

Without God in his life King Saul went downhill and allowed bad temper to rule him. (How is your temper these days?) He was so depressed his servants suggested he hire someone to play music to soothe him. One servant said, ''I saw one of Jesse's sons, a skillful musician, a man of courage, careful in his speech and attractive.'' It was our friend David. Read that again. What a record! How would you be described? Saul sent for him and so David began to work in the very palace where he would one day be king. God was ordering David's life, step by step.

AUGUST 7   1 SAMUEL 17:1-11

Just then a war started. The army of the Israelis was set up on one mountain and the Philistines opposite. Suddenly out from the Philistines came a great giant over nine feet tall, wearing a heavy coat of armour and carrying a huge spear. He roared across the valley, ''Hey, Israel! I have a great idea. Instead of everyone going to battle, just send one of your chaps to fight me and whoever wins decides the war. Come on, cowards. Send out a man... I dare you!'' Guess who were sitting shivering in their tents with the flaps down? Every Israeli man right up to King Saul. Is the situation hopeless? No. God has a man.

AUGUST 8   1 SAMUEL 17:12-27

David was back home tending his father's sheep. Jesse said, ''David, go and see how your brothers are and take them some of our good food.'' Notice that David (1) obeyed his father, (2) rose early to do it, (3) left a man to care for the sheep. As he reached the war area out came Goliath shouting his challenge, and again the Israelis ran in fear. But David was not afraid; he was angry. ''Who is he to defy the armies of the living God?'' he said. David had the right picture; Goliath was defying God because Israel was God's people. If you belong to God then what happens to you concerns Him.

AUGUST 9   1 SAMUEL 17:28-39

David's words were told to Saul and he sent for him. In the king's presence David repeated, "Don't be afraid because of Goliath for I will fight him." Saul was astonished. "Why you are just a lad!" he said, "and Goliath has been a soldier for years!" But David replied, "I keep my father's sheep. Once a lion and a bear came and stole a lamb and I took the bear by his beard and killed him. The lion too. The same God who helped me then will help me now." David was not sure of himself; he was sure of God. Psalm 91:2 states, "in Him will I trust."

AUGUST 10   1 SAMUEL 17:40-58

Saul offered David his suit of armour. David tried it on - and took it off. Instead he chose five smooth stones for his sling shot. How would you like to fight a nine foot giant with a slingshot? Goliath was insulted when he saw David and he roared, "I'll give your remains to the birds!" David replied, "The Lord will give *you* to me." Then he *ran* toward Goliath, swinging his slingshot over his head and let the stone go full blast. It struck Goliath in his forehead, stunned him and he fell to the ground. David ran up, took Goliath's own sword and cut off his head. With God's help and the use of what he had, David killed a man who had terrified the whole Israeli army.

AUGUST 11   1 SAMUEL 18:1-11

Think of your best friend. How much do you love this friend? When Prince Jonathan met David the Bible says he loved David as much as he loved himself. That's a whopping amount because we really love ourselves. Jonathan loved David so much he wanted to give him all he had. But King Saul had become jealous of David since he killed Goliath. Saul's jealousy led him to try to kill David. Song of Solomon 8:6 states, "Love is strong as death; jealousy is cruel as the grave." Let love rule.

AUGUST 12   1 SAMUEL 18:12-21

David was now a famous person and so was closely watched by everyone. Each day the people saw what he did, where he went and how he acted. (How would you like a record kept of everything you did and said for even a day?) The Bible says David behaved wisely and the result of this was that the people loved him. But more important, twice in these verses it states God was with him. Can people see that God is with you because of how you live?

AUGUST 13   1 SAMUEL 18:22-30

Did you ever notice that when things go wrong in your life it is always someone else's fault? Saul was like that with David. He offered David his daughter Michal as wife, for a price... one hundred dead Philistines. Saul hoped the Philistines would kill David instead, and that would take care of David. He thought by doing this his troubles would be over. He was willing to use his own daughter - risk other lives - anything rather than face the fact that his problem was himself. Take a long look in the mirror and admit that the person facing you is the cause of most of your trouble. Ask God for help.

AUGUST 14   1 SAMUEL 19:1-7

Saul was so desparate to get rid of David he even told his son Jonathan to kill him. But remember Jonathan loved David. Jonathan's thought was to protect David and he quickly told him to leave the palace and hide. Jonathan did not stop there, but had the courage to go to his father and reason with him. As they stood together he said, "Why do you try to kill David? He has done nothing to you, in fact, he helped you by killing Goliath when everyone else was terrified. You were happy with him then. Don't hurt an innocent man." Jonathan spoke for his friend David, and praised him. What kind of friend are you?

AUGUST 15   1 SAMUEL 19:8-17

But once a-gain Saul's jealousy overcame him and again he tried to kill David. Again David escaped - this time to his own home. Saul sent men to wait outside to kill David in the morning, but Michal told him he must leave at once. That night she quietly let David down through a window and he fled. Then she rolled up a a blanket and put it in the bed with a pillow of goat's hair. When the men came in to take David she said, "He's sick." Saul told them to go back and bring David bed and all. But when they forced their way into the room - there was only a roll of blankets in the bed. Do you get the feeling God was looking after David? Do you know nothing can touch you unless God allows it?

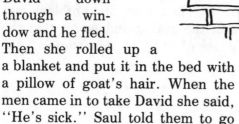

AUGUST 16   1 SAMUEL 19:18-24

Saul did not give up easily. He sent more servants to search for David and finally went himself. Let us consider three things about David: (1) God was watching over him; (2) he had at least three people who were willing to risk their own lives for him - Jonathan - Michal - and now Samuel; (3)

we do not read of any complaints from David. Day after day he was pursued by a murderous king. Yet no complaints. No crying. No lying on the floor and kicking the heels. How many times did you complain yesterday, and about what? The Bible asks, "Why does a living man complain?"

AUGUST 17   1 SAMUEL 20:1-10

David asked Jonathan, "What harm have I done to your father? Why does he want to kill me?" Jonathan was distressed because he knew David was innocent. The Bible says about the Lord Jesus, "they hated Him without a cause." When the people demanded His death, even Pilate said, "Why? What wrong has He done?" Our Lord's life was perfect. He did only good; He hurt no one. Yet this perfect, holy Person allowed Himself to be hanged on a cross, for us. How can we do anything but worship Him?

AUGUST 18   1 SAMUEL 20:11-23

Jonathan was willing to help David all he could and together they formed a plan. It was holiday time and all the king's servants, including David, would be expected at the palace. When Saul noticed David's absence, Jonathan planned

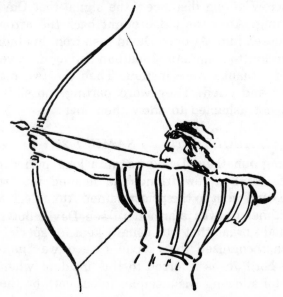

to "cover up" for him. If Saul said nothing, it would be safe for David to come out of hiding. If Saul was angry, David was to stay where he was. The signal was an arrow. If Jonathan shot the arrow short, all was well; but if long - go! David agreed. He would accept whatever God had for him, good or bad.

AUGUST 19   1 SAMUEL 20:24-34

Saul noticed David's absence, but said nothing. The next day when David did not come, Saul said, "Where is the son of Jesse?" He would not even call David by name. Jonathan gave his excuse, at which Saul blew up. He was furious. When Jonathan defended David, Saul picked up his spear and flung it at his own son! Jonathan left in deep anger. Notice why. He was grieved for David, not for himself. Genuine unselfish feeling. Any of this around you lately?

AUGUST 20   1 SAMUEL 20:35-42

Jonathan now had to let David know the bad news. Saul wanted David dead. So Jonathan took a bow and arrows and went with a young lad to the field where David hid. He then shot an arrow a long distance - the signal that David had to keep running. After the lad brought back the arrows, Jonathan dismissed him. At once David rose from his hiding place and bowed low to Jonathan. Jonathan had again saved his life and David's thanks were instant. Then the two men kissed each other and cried. They were parting, possibly forever, and were not ashamed to show their love.

AUGUST 21   1 SAMUEL 21:1-7

Leaving Jonathan, David began a long period of hiding from Saul. With a few friends he headed into the bush. Hungry, David went to the priest named Ahimelech to ask for bread. Ahimelech was alarmed to see David but gave him what he had - bread that was usually kept for special services. Ahimelech recognized that David's need was more important. The Lord Jesus referred to this incident when He was criticized for allowing His disciples to eat corn on the sabbath

(Luke 6:1-5). The Lord said that He was more important than any day. Do you have the important things in the right order? Is Christ first?

AUGUST 22   1 SAMUEL 21:8-15

David - who killed Goliath with a slingshot - now felt he needed a sword. So Ahimelech gave him the sword that was there - Goliath's own. David, who had such confidence in God, now ran for fear of Saul. David, who was described in verse 18 of chapter 16 as a prudent man, now was in such a panic that he pretended to be crazy. This is David, the man who "behaved himself wisely" because "the Lord was with him?" What had happened? He was out of touch with God. It's no different with us. Lose touch with God and you make a complete mess of your life.

AUGUST 23   1 SAMUEL 22:1-8

Psalm 57:1 says, "in the shadow of thy wings will I make my refuge." The heading of the psalm states that David wrote this in the cave. Here is a new man. He is back in touch with God. Now his relatives, friends and people who were discouraged or upset came to join him in the cave. Even his parents arrived. Notice David took particular care of them. He asked the king of Moab if they could live there until David knew what God's plans were for him. What have you done for your parents lately... or ever? The Bible says, "Honour thy father and thy mother." They are your special care.

AUGUST 24   1 SAMUEL 22:9-16

Meantime, back at the palace, Saul had grown worse. He could think of nothing but getting rid of David. Now he accused his servants of conspiring against him. At this point Doeg spoke up. Doeg had been in Ahimelech's house when he gave David bread. So he told Saul all that Ahimelech had done, and added a bit to the story. Saul was roaring mad and sent for Ahimelech. Ahimelech told Saul that David was a faithful servant. This so enraged Saul that he said, "For that you and all the priests will die." Saul's disobedience and jealousy have caused him to order the death of God's servants. Could this happen to us? See James 3:16. "For where envying and strife is, there is confusion and *every evil work.*"

AUGUST 25   1 SAMUEL 22:17-23

Saul then said to his servants, "Kill the priests of the Lord!" But notice the reaction of his servants. They refused. Put yourself in like position. A powerful person orders you to do something you know is wrong. What would happen? Acts 5:29 states, "We ought to obey God rather than men." Saul went wildly on. Turning to Doeg he ordered him to do it. Instantly Doeg began, and finally killed every priest in the area. Why would God put up with that? The Bible says He will surely punish wicked men when their time comes. Saul's end was approaching.

AUGUST 26   1 SAMUEL 23:1-12

David, still living in the bush, heard that the Philistines had attacked Israel. He said, "Too bad." No. He said, "Maybe someone will do something." No. He asked God if he and his friends should go and help. Right! And God said yes. But David's friends were afraid to go, so David asked God again. This time they took God at His word and went to the battle. As God had promised, they defeated the  enemy. Three times in these verses we read, "David enquired of the Lord." That's the secret of success.

AUGUST 27   1 SAMUEL 23:13-18

Imagine having someone trying to kill you every day of your life. That's how it was with David. Verse 14 says Saul looked for him *every day.* But see the other part of the verse.

God did not allow Saul to get to David. David did not have to worry for five minutes. He was in God's care. Regardless of how desperate your situation seems, God is in control of everything. Remember that.

AUGUST 28   1 SAMUEL 23:19-29

Saul heard that David was hiding in a place called Maon. So he raced off with his army to find him. Picture a mountain. Saul and his men reach it from the south and go stomping around it on the right side. David and his men reach it from the north and go around the opposite way, so they completely missed each other. Just luck? Not with God. Once again He has taken care of David.

AUGUST 29   1 SAMUEL 24:1-8

Finally David had his chance to get even. Saul and an army of 3,000 men were combing the country to find David. Saul stopped in a cave to rest, unaware that David and his men stood silently in the dark all around the inside of the cave, watching him. One of David's men whispered, "Now is your chance to kill Saul!" David crept quietly over to Saul, lifted his sword and... cut off part of Saul's robe. His robe? He didn't kill him? No, and afterward David even regretted cutting the robe. Saul was still king and therefore represented authority. All authority is established by God and David wanted no part of rebelling against it.

AUGUST 30   1 SAMUEL 24:9-16

Saul left the cave and suddenly he heard a voice behind him saying, "My lord the king!" When he whirled around, there was David bowing to him in the mouth of the cave. David held up the part of Saul's robe he had cut off and said, "See, I could have killed you just now. Why do you hunt me? I wish you no harm." Saul was shaken. He called, "Is that you, David my son?" and he burst into tears. David had addressed Saul with respect and acted with honour. The effect was to make Saul so ashamed he cried. Are you the first to stop quarreling? Proverbs 20:3 states, "It is an honour for a man to cease from strife."

AUGUST 31   1 SAMUEL 24:17-22

Saul admitted to David, "You are a better person than I. I have been rotten to you and you have repaid me with kindness." (Could anyone say that to you?) Saul said any other person would have killed him, but David had actually saved his life. "I know one day you will be king," he said. "Promise you will be kind to my family." And David promised. What a man! Yet Saul promised David nothing. He wanted all the giving to come from David. Are you a taker or a giver? Do you take everything from God, but give nothing in return?

SEPTEMBER 1   JAMES 1:1-8

James is writing this letter to the many Jewish Christians who had moved away from their homes because of the persecution they were facing. Other Jews were persecuting them because they had accepted the Lord Jesus Christ as their Saviour. This letter would be handed from person to person rather than read in public. He encourages them to accept trials as opportunities to exercise their faith. We exercise our bodies by swimming, cycling, walking, etc., and at times our faith is exercised (or further developed) by trials that challenge it. James also encouraged them to ask God for wisdom. When trials enter our lives we should immediately ask the Lord to give us wisdom and understanding. Trials can be brought about by ourselves or they can come from outside sources. Try to think of examples of both.

SEPTEMBER 2   JAMES 1:9-15

Do you ever blame God when things go wrong? Not that you shake your fist and say, "God, you made me do that!" But have you ever done something wrong and thought - "Well, why didn't God stop me from doing wrong?" There really isn't too much difference, is there? James says it clearly: he says, God does not tempt us to do evil but we are tempted by our own evil desires. When we give in to those desires, we sin. The temptation is not the sin but the giving in to the temptation is sin. When Eve encouraged Adam to eat of the forbidden fruit it wasn't sinful until he ate it. He could have said no! He gave in to an evil desire! Let us resist those desires before they cause us to sin.

SEPTEMBER 3   JAMES 1:16-21

Look again at verse 17. Did you notice the confidence James has in God? He emphasizes that God does not change. For people who were suffering because they were Christians this was very important to understand. They were going through awful situations and it would be easy to think that God had forgotten them. When your circumstances have changed, have you ever thought that God has changed? Satan wants you to believe that God does change. *HE DOES NOT!* The Scriptures say: "I am the Lord, I change not" (Malachi 3:6). Hebrews 13:8 says: "Jesus Christ, the same yesterday and today and forever." James encourages them to build their understanding on the Word of God, not on their feelings or circumstances. This is important for us too. What do you think of verse 19? Ask the Lord to help you put it into practice today!

SEPTEMBER 4   JAMES 1:22-27

If you were going out with a friend and, looking in a mirror, you noticed your face was dirty, you would wash it, wouldn't you? If you looked in a mirror and saw that both your eyes were very swollen, you would probably go to a doctor. You would do something about it! How often have you read the Bible, seen something you needed to change in your life, and then ignored it? This book you are reading is called "The Looking Glass" because it encourages you to read the Word of God to see reflections of yourself in it. Yesterday the Word told us not to become angry. Did you do something about it or did you just put down *THE MIRROR* and forget? The importance of hearing or reading the Scriptures is not how often we read it but how obedient we are to it. Today James tells us a way by which we can fool ourselves. What is it?

SEPTEMBER 5   JAMES 2:1-7

So many people think that God really loves those who are rich - or they wouldn't be rich! Do you think God works that way? Think of the riches of Christ before He left His Father's throne to come to earth. Did God love Him more when He was surrounded by His riches and majesty than He did when Christ lived on the earth and didn't even have a home of His own? Of course not! Why do we act differently toward people who are rich than we do toward those who are poor? If we are impressed with a person's wealth we have the wrong motives. The importance is the person - not what he has or has not! Be honest with yourself as you meet people. Do not be impressed with what they have but with what they are!

SEPTEMBER 6   JAMES 2:8-13

Have you ever wondered who loves you most? You don't have to give that too much thought if you are honest. YOU do! This is true of us all. No one loves us as much as we love ourselves. Today the Scriptures remind us that we are to love our neighbour as much as we love ourselves. A neighbour isn't just the person who lives next door to you but those people you spend so much time with at school. Do you love them as much as you love yourself? Be honest now. The perfect example of love, of course, is the Lord Jesus Christ. He loved His enemies more than He loved Himself. He proved this as He died for our sins. Please remember that Jesus Christ did not die as a martyr. He willingly chose to be God's sacrifice for us. No one can love his neighbour as himself without accepting God's love for him which was proven when Christ died and rose alive from the dead.

SEPTEMBER 7   JAMES 2:14-26

Many people misunderstand this passage of Scripture. James is saying that people who put their faith in God prove it by their good works. He is not saying if you do good works you are accepted by God. God's idea of good works is what you do because of your faith. Perhaps you accepted Christ as your Saviour when you were at camp. Have people who know you well seen a difference in you or have you just told them about your great faith? Faith is trusting in what God says. Good works are the results of that trust.

SEPTEMBER 8   JAMES 3:1-12

Have you ever carried a rattle snake in your pocket? It isn't really the thing to do, is it? Some people like snakes but no one would carry a rattle snake as a pet because it is filled with deadly poison. You say - "But it may never bite you." That is true but who is willing to take that risk? James tells us that the tongue is full of deadly poison. Do you agree with him? Perhaps not now when you are quietly reading the Bible but what about the time you were blamed for something you did not do? Or the time you were playing a game and someone tripped you purposely? Were you able to control your tongue? Don't kill anyone's love or respect for you by the poisonous thoughts your tongue can express. Ask the Lord to control your thoughts and to keep your tongue from speaking anything that would dishonour Him.

SEPTEMBER 9   JAMES 3:13-18

Verse 17 is one you should consider thoroughly and memorize. So many people are interested in being worldly-wise. They want to know the wisest way to make a lot of money, to become popular, or powerful, or successful. They seek the wisest way to keep healthy, to travel, to work, to out-do another person without them knowing. These things do take the wisdom of the world but James speaks of the wisdom from above. The Living Bible defines it so well! First of all it is pure, full of quiet gentleness, peace-loving, courteous; it allows discussion and is full of mercy and good deeds; it is wholehearted, straightforward and sincere. Try to imagine what a wonderful place the world would be if each of us had, and used, the wisdom that comes from above! It could start with you! Are you interested?

SEPTEMBER 10   JAMES 4:1-10

Sometimes it is difficult to know the reasons behind our actions. In many cases it involves selfish motives. We want things our way for our benefit. James tells us that this is how the people of the world react. If we claim to be Christians we should not be reacting the way the world does. We are instructed to resist the devil. We must fight against his ways and when we do he runs away from us.We can do this as we become more acquainted with God's Word and realize that the Holy Spirit will help us to resist the devil. As we draw nearer to the Lord we find He draws nearer to us. Let Him win in your life today - over selfish ways and attacks from the devil.

SEPTEMBER 11   JAMES 4:11-17

It is so easy to see the faults in other people, isn't it? We judge people so quickly and yet if we were to do the same thing we would think of a good reason to believe it was right for us. Do you find it easier to give a compliment or to criticize a person? Sometimes we control our tongue by not criticizing and we think we are great. Perhaps we should have used our tongue to give a compliment or a word of encouragement. We should be careful to know control in both areas. Isn't that what verse 17 brings to our attention?

SEPTEMBER 12   JAMES 5:1-11

Some people think that the Bible criticizes people who are rich. It does not. The Scriptures teach the proper use and value of money and riches. If you become rich at the cost of another person God will never honour you. At times it might be necessary for you, as a Christian, to show much patience to some who misuse you to better themselves. James reminds us that our minds must be on the Lord who shows pity and tender mercy. The Lord is in control and as you trust your life to Him, He will handle any who cause you hurt or harm.

SEPTEMBER 13   JAMES 5:12-20

Do you think you are too old to go to church or that the church is old-fashioned and hasn't anything to offer you?

Read this passage again and see how much the church can help you. We do not speak of a building, of course, but the people who, knowing God through faith in Christ, make up the church. Spending time with other Christians is very important. To have people pray with you and for you is necessary. To have those who love you enough to correct you is a great privilege. You need the church and others in the church need you.

SEPTEMBER 14   PSALM 45:1-17

This Psalm may be difficult for you to understand. Sometimes it is considered a song of love. Throughout Scripture the church is spoken of as the bride of Christ. As you read this passage think of it as the church expressing her love to the Lord Jesus Christ. One day Christ will come to this earth to take the church to be in God's presence with Him. Again, we do not speak of a building but of the people who make up the church - those who have accepted Christ as their Saviour. Are you part of His church? Could you write a psalm of love to the Lord?

SEPTEMBER 15   PSALM 46:1-11

Do you ever feel that everything has gone wrong and you might fall apart? If you memorize Psalm 46 it could be a great help to you when you feel that way. We live in a very busy world and each of us needs a refuge - not a crutch - but a place of protection and strength. We can find this in God! He is in control of the entire world and each detail of our lives. Often we are so busy that we forget this and become trapped with fears or questions or unbelief. The Psalmist says, "Be still and know that I am God!" When you do this, you know that He is with you and that He is your refuge. Memorize verses 10 and 11.

SEPTEMBER 16   DEUTERONOMY 1:1-8

Moses had led the Israelis from Egypt toward the land which God had promised them. The distance was not very great but because of disobedience to the Lord it took them forty years to make the journey. Most of the people Moses was speaking to were born during that forty-year period. You may find that parts of Deuteronomy seem to repeat things you have read in the first four books of the Bible. That is true. Moses repeats much of the law given to him by God because these people were very young when it was first given. Before they entered the land God promised to give them, Moses made sure they understood the Lord's commandments to them.

SEPTEMBER 17   DEUTERONOMY 1:9-18

Moses begins to recall the story of their forty years of travelling. It is interesting that he begins by reflecting his own feelings. Moses always remembered that he was just a man and knew that it was impossible for him to handle all these people by himself. He very carefully shared his responsibilities with wise men who were well known. The problems of the people were handled by them and Moses was free to take care of any serious situation. He didn't think he was the only one who could do the job.

SEPTEMBER 18   DEUTERONOMY 1:19-28

You probably know some people who do not trust God. This was true of many of these Israelis. Moses sent twelve men ahead of the others to spy out the land. Two of them were really excited about it and said they should go ahead and trust the Lord to take care of them, but the ten others were full of complaints and fears. As usual, it was the discouragements that spread throughout the people, not the encouragements. It is easy to become discouraged with the things God tells us to do if we think we do them by ourselves. He never expects us to do anything without knowing He is with us to help. Next time you are discouraged, question whether you are doing things your way or God's way with His strength.

SEPTEMBER 19   DEUTERONOMY 1:29-40

Moses reminds these young people that only two people of all the thousands who left Egypt would enter the land God had promised them. Not even Moses went into that land! The two who did were Caleb and Joshua. These were the two men who came back and reported to the Israelis that they should not be afraid. God had promised them the land and He would be with them as they went in to claim it. The people did not listen. God did not allow them to enter Canaan, but the two who believed God received all that He promised.

SEPTEMBER 20   DEUTERONOMY 1:41-46

Do you wonder why the Israelis were disobedient when God said not to go and fight against the Amorites? God gave this message to Moses and he gave it clearly to the people. Notice verse 43, Moses said - "So I spoke to you, but you would not listen." Do you always listen when you are spoken to? It is easy to pretend we did not hear, isn't it? especially when it is something we really do not want to do. God speaks to you today through His Word. Please listen - and obey! Remember verse 45.

SEPTEMBER 21   DEUTERONOMY 2:1-15

You will notice that the directions given in this reading are very clear. You may not know the areas mentioned but it is easy to understand that they were clearly instructed. So often we make simple things difficult. As you read the Bible be careful not to do this. The Lord told the Israelis to trust Him and not to be afraid but again and again they doubted His Word and would not trust Him. Can this be said of you?

SEPTEMBER 22   DEUTERONOMY 2:16-25

Sometimes at school there will be one boy who is very strong and always wanting to fight. Stories are told of him and soon many people are afraid of him even though they do not know him or have reason to be afraid. The other nations were afraid of the Israelis but not because they were great fighters. They were not. The people were afraid of them because God was with them and as they obeyed His orders their battles were won. This is true of the Christian today as well.

SEPTEMBER 23   DEUTERONOMY 2:26-37

We have further proof in today's reading of God's Presence with the Israelis as they chose to obey Him. Why do you find it so hard to obey God? Is it because you cannot see Him or touch Him? Or could it be that someone has told you the Bible is not true? Whatever the reason, you should think seriously about it. To believe what God says means to exercise faith. If we could see or touch God we would not need faith. He calls on us to believe that He is - and we prove that we believe Him when we obey Him.

SEPTEMBER 24   DEUTERONOMY 3:1-7

Sometimes when you read Scripture it appears that God is unjust in His ways. Today you have read that all the people of Bashan were killed. These people were not only the enemies of the Israelis but they were God's enemies. If you are a Christian you have enemies in your life - not Og, the king of Bashan - but other enemies. Read Ephesians 6, verse 12. Paul reminds us that our enemies are not flesh and blood but the rulers and powers of world darkness and the spiritual forces of wickedness. Take the time to read verses 12 to 18 of Ephesians 6 because this is the way the Christian is protected. Remember these are also God's enemies and He wants to fight for you.

SEPTEMBER 25   DEUTERONOMY 3:8-29

Moses did not go into the promised land. He wanted to, and asked God to allow him, but God said he could not. (Numbers 20:12 explains why.) He was allowed to go to a very high mountain and view the land. Then God told him to speak to Joshua and encourage him because he would be the leader who took the Israelis across Jordan. Moses was to strengthen and encourage Joshua and give him the leadership which had been his for the previous forty years. Do you think this would be difficult for Moses? Read Numbers 27: 18-23.

SEPTEMBER 26   DEUTERONOMY 4:1-13

Remember that Moses knows he will die in a very short time. His last forty years were spent leading the Israelis in God's ways, as well as to the land God promised them. Before he dies he is very anxious to give them as much instruction as possible. He reminds them clearly of their need to be grounded in God's Word. He explains that they should not add to it

or take from it. He tells them that keeping God's Word is the strength of a nation. Pay attention to this passage of Scripture because it is as necessary today as it was then. It is our responsibility to pray for those who are in authority in our country. Wouldn't it be great if our nation was directed by the principles of Scripture?

SEPTEMBER 27   DEUTERONOMY 4:14-24

Moses emphasizes the need to follow God's Word in their new land. He tells them if they don't they could easily begin to worship idols. When you are at camp it is very easy for you to read the Bible, to pray and to share your thoughts of God with others but then when you return home, you find it difficult. Perhaps it is because you do not have a Christian family or friends. Please realize how necessary it is for you to read God's Word daily and to be directed by Him. If you become careless you could allow other things or people to take His place in your life. Pay particular attention to verse 24 but balance it with John 3:16.

SEPTEMBER 28   DEUTERONOMY 4:25-31

It was mentioned earlier that the people Moses was speaking to were all under forty years of age, other than Caleb and Joshua. Some people think that to read the Bible and to pray is only good for children. God does not think that way. Moses reminds these young people that when they have grandchildren and great grandchildren they should still put God, His Word and His ways first in their lives. Memorize verse 31 and think about it during the day.

SEPTEMBER 29   DEUTERONOMY 4:32-40

Verse 34 shows ways by which God proved Himself to the Israelis. Verse 35 tells us why. Have you ever listed the ways God has proven Himself to you? Moses reminds them of the trials, wars and terrors, as well as the signs, wonders, mighty and outstretched hand. Have you ever thought that God proved Himself only by good things? This is not so. God is always with us, in everything, and this proves to us the extent of His love and power. Memorize verse 35 - it will help you in times of difficulty. Remember - "the Lord, *HE IS GOD;* there is none else beside Him."

SEPTEMBER 30   DEUTERONOMY 4:41-49

In the days of Joshua there were cities that were especially used as cities of refuge (or protection). If a person killed another by accident he would go to one of these cities to live. As long as he lived there other people could not harm him for his mistake. Have you realized that you need a place of protection? We need a refuge from our sin and guilt before our Holy God. As Moses provided cities of refuge, God also provides a refuge. God's refuge for you is the Lord Jesus Christ. His death and resurrection for our sins provides us with protection from God's punishment. He was our sacrifice before God. Do you know Christ as your refuge?

OCTOBER 1   DEUTERONOMY 5:1-11

You and I applaud and cheer for our camp when it competes in sports with another camp. We may even go farther and become jealous when another camp shows itself better than we are in some way. That jealousy is childish. See Luke 15:27-32.

Why, then, does God call Himself "jealous" (verse 9)? Because nothing else is *really* like God. He is one and only. He alone has created us and will bring us to Heaven. All other gods are fake. So He jealously guards His rights in order that people might share the blessings of the eternal life which comes only from Him. God's jealousy is not suspicious or childish. It is a part of His love for His creatures.

OCTOBER 2   DEUTERONOMY 5:12-21

We all admire at some time the things that other people own. A coat, a bike, a football. When that admiration becomes a desire to get those things by almost any means, it becomes coveting or greediness. See verse 21. We today do not make wooden and metal idols and call them "gods." But the Bible says coveting is putting something else in God's place (Colossians 3:5). Such greed often leads to the other sins of verses 12 to 20.

OCTOBER 3   DEUTERONOMY 5:22-33

Coming face to face with the glory and greatness of God was a scary experience for the people of Israel (verse 25). It is strange that you and I are so careless about God's words in the Bible. Do you think we are careless because we have not seen His greatness or heard His voice?

The Lord Jesus once said, "If you have seen me, you have seen the Father" (John 14:9). We can understand what God is like by reading the Bible stories about His Son. And that's a lot less scary than what happened on the mountain (Deuteronomy 5:22). But God's commands are just as firm when they come through Jesus Christ as when they came from the mountain. Compare Deuteronomy 5:32,33 with Matthew 7:21.

OCTOBER 4   DEUTERONOMY 6:1-9

The Lord's commands always come to us with a promise. In verses 1-3 the Israelites are promised the good land of Palestine, if they make the Lord the centre of their lives (verses 4, 5).

The Lord Jesus promised joy to His disciples if they followed His commands (John 15:10,11). Sometimes we modern disciples of Christ try to get the blessings of God without carrying out the commands. It can't be done!

OCTOBER 5   DEUTERONOMY 6:10-15

Write down all the good things that God has given you. Things that you didn't get by your own doing. Your good health. Your time at camp last summer. At least one other person who loves you. These are some of the things that might be on your list. Maybe you will be surprised how long the list will be.

The Israelites are not alone in receiving from God what they had not laboured for (verses 10,11). The greatest blessing from God is everlasting life. It also comes to us apart from our own doing. See Ephesians 2:8,9 and 1 Peter 1:18,19.

OCTOBER 6   DEUTERONOMY 6:16-25

When the young Israelite of a later time would ask his

parents the meaning of God's laws, he would receive an unusual answer (verses 21-23). One of the reasons for the laws was that God's mighty deeds would be brought to memory. Those deeds had meant the salvation of the Israelites from slavery in Egypt.

Christians likewise have something to remind them of what God has done for them. Christ left us a supper to observe. See 1 Corinthians 11:23-26. That supper reminds us that He died on the cross to save us from Hell and to bring us to Heaven.

OCTOBER 7   DEUTERONOMY 7:1-8

These verses do not provide an example of how we are to treat foreigners or those of other races. God was using Israel to bring His punishment upon very wicked peoples. Later He would use foreigners to bring His punishment upon Israel (Jeremiah 25:8-11).

What the passage does tell us is that God's people belong to Him because He loves them (verses 6-8). In our day God's people are the Christians. Once a person has come into God's family by receiving Christ as Saviour, "enemies" must be overcome if that person is to live to the full his new life in that family. Some of the enemies are the temptations that Christians face. Like the enemies of Israel, the Christian's enemies are cleared away with God's help (Deuteronomy 7:1; 1 Corinthians 10:13).

OCTOBER 8   DEUTERONOMY 7:9-16

God is faithful. He will not go back on His promises. He kept His word with Israel. He will keep it in your case, too. Read Hebrews 13:5,6,8. Jesus our Lord never changes. He it is who said to His followers, "I will be with you always, even to the end of the world" (Matthew 28:20).

OCTOBER 9   DEUTERONOMY 7:17-26

Have you ever trembled in your heart and thought, "The things I have to face are much too big for me"? And you were probably right. They are too big for you. But not too big for God. The Apostle Paul learned to face problems and troubles with God's help. He wrote, "I can do all things through Christ who strengthens me" (Philippians 4:13). That is the lesson the Lord sought to teach Israel (verses 18, 21, 23). Let Him teach it to you, too.

OCTOBER 10   DEUTERONOMY 8:1-10

If we could arrange the world to suit us, we would probably get rid of discipline. We would be careful to keep the pleasant things, such as those in verses 7 to 10. But the rigourous features of life would be out.

And how much poorer we would be if we did get rid of discipline! Our spiritual "muscles" are toughened by the spiritual exercises of trust, hope, love, and devotion to the Lord. To be genuine disciples of Christ we must enter His discipline so that we may learn to live not only by "bread" but by what He says to us (verse 3).

OCTOBER 11   DEUTERONOMY 8:11-20

It may be news to you that you must take care not to forget God. When life is a problem, we quickly ask God to help us solve our difficulties. When we do not have the things we need, we pray that the Lord will supply them. (Things we need, not just things we want.) Surely we shall never forget God. Yet, when life is going well, forgetting God is a temptation (verses 12-14). Have you left God out of your life today?

OCTOBER 12

DEUTERONOMY 9:1-6

"Little Jack Horner" is a nursery rhyme we might have learned when we were small. Jack was pleased with himself because he had done something important. He had found a plum in the pie. Don't be a spiritual "Jack Horner." God sent His Son to save you, not because you are such a nice person, but

because He loves you. See verse 4; Deuteronomy 7:7,8; John 3:16. Remember, the Israelites were not the only stubborn people who ever lived (verse 6).

OCTOBER 13   DEUTERONOMY 10:1-9

The tribe of Levi was special. They were given a special job: to carry the sacred box, or ark, and to serve in the Lord's temple. No one else was given the privilege of serving God in the way the Levites did.

Although you and I are not Levites, God has also given special jobs to us. No one has the same situation in life that you have. No one has exactly the same set of friends, the same opportunities, or the same problems. Others may have similar ones, but not the same. Since no one else is quite like you, you have a special job to serve the Lord where you are.

OCTOBER 14   DEUTERONOMY 10:10-22

Even the best human beings may disappoint us. Even the best people forget promises made. Or they are not always fair when they mete out punishment or give rewards. God is not like that. He is always fair. He loves important and unimportant people. He provides for the great and the small. God never changes, and that is comforting to know.

There is another side. Since God is always fair, we cannot trick Him into favouring us over someone else. Or, we cannot fool Him into thinking we are obedient when we have sinned. The Lord is a God greatly to be loved and greatly to be respected.

OCTOBER 15   DEUTERONOMY 11:1-9

The Israelites had witnessed the wondrous action of God in their own lives (verses 2, 7). Perhaps the reason your Christian faith seems so dull is that you have never seen God at work in your life. Your faith is a second-hand religion. It is really your parents' faith, or your camp counsellor's faith.

Now, second-hand chairs may be refinished so that they become quite usable. Second-hand religion is all but useless. Do you, then, know personally that Jesus is your Saviour and

Lord? Has He taught you wonderful things from His Bible? Or have you just heard others talk of such things?

OCTOBER 16   DEUTERONOMY 11:10-17

Throughout their history, the Israelites would be tempted to worship and serve gods other than the Lord. The gods of the land which Israel was entering were gods who were supposed to bring fruitful harvests. Israel was to remember that it was really the Lord who sent the rains (verse 14) and caused the grass to grow (verse 15).

You may work hard at your paper route or babysitting. Even so, remember it is the Lord who gives you the good health to do the work.

OCTOBER 17   DEUTERONOMY 11:18-25

You don't see people today with portions of the Bible tied to their hands or foreheads (verse 18). But you may still see Bible texts on the walls of homes and church buildings. You may have even made such a plaque at camp.

Still the best way to impress God's words upon our minds is the old way mentioned in verse 18: to memorize it. Of course, there is more to verses 18-20 than mere memorization. The purpose in knowing God's words by heart is that our hearts and lives will be affected by those words (verse 22). Read James 1:22 and Psalm 119:11.

OCTOBER 18   DEUTERONOMY 11:26-32

What a lopsided choice! A blessing or a curse. Who in his right mind would choose a curse? Strange enough, that is exactly what Israel did choose as the years passed. Oh, it did not appear as a curse. It looked like a blessing to worship all those false gods. Similarly, the temptations of the devil seem attractive to us, not the curse that they actually are.

God's way, however hard it may appear, is always best.

OCTOBER 19   DEUTERONOMY 12:1-12

When Jesus began to tell people about God's kingdom, He did not command them to burn the synagogues of the Jews. When Paul the apostle told the Gentiles the gospel, he did not urge them to demolish the temples of Athens, Ephesus, or Corinth. Why did God command Israel to destroy the altars and worship centres of the nations in the Promised Land? Part of the answer is that Israel was carrying out God's sentence of punishment upon very wicked people. (See the note for October 7.)

The Lord also commanded Israel to sacrifice to Him. Notice that He gave certain directions about how to sacrifice and where (verses 11,12). God has likewise given us clear instructions to meet for worship with other Christians. Read Hebrews 10:25; 1 Corinthians 11:23-26.

OCTOBER 20   DEUTERONOMY 12:29-32

To neglect to take a compass on a cross-country camping trip might endanger everyone in your cabin group. To take away from what God has said in His Word is dangerous spiritually. "Oh, I can still be a Christian even if I don't attend church or Sunday school," we may think. But we are taking away from the lesson we learned from yesterday's passage.

To add to what God has said is also unadvisable. Eve did that. (Compare Genesis 2:16,17 with 3:2,3.) The Pharisees in Jesus' day had done it. (See Mark 7:7,8.) Can you think of ways that we add to what God has said?

OCTOBER 21   DEUTERONOMY 13:1-5

Long ago the Lord God spoke to men through prophets and dreamers. Not all prophets and dreamers were the Lord's men. Some were fakes. These verses tell how to test whether a prophet was true or false.

Today the Lord speaks to men through the Bible and those who teach us the Bible. The test for the Bible is the same as that for the prophets of old: does what the Bible says come true? The test for those who teach the Bible is: do they tell us what the Bible really says?

OCTOBER 22 DEUTERONOMY 14:22-29

As you grow older you are finding that money is very important in life. You may receive an allowance from your parents. You may have a paper route or another kind of job. How you use the money you earn tends to show what kind of a Christian you are.

The Israelites were commanded to set aside a part of what they earned. That part, or tithe, was to be the Lord's. Do you give part of your earnings to God by putting it in the collection plate at church or Sunday school? Or do you keep it all for yourself?

OCTOBER 23 DEUTERONOMY 15:1-11

Setting aside a tithe of our money is not the only way of using our earnings for God. Other people may not have as much as we do. If they need help to get food and clothing, we should share what we have (verse 11). Perhaps a good project for your Sunday school class or boys' or girls' club would be to help an orphan boy or girl overseas who does not have enough to eat.

OCTOBER 24 DEUTERONOMY 15:12-18

The ancient Hebrews lived in a world where slavery was practised. A means was provided every seven years to set the slaves free (verse 12). In other times and places slaves were slaves for life. God has given you and me so much that we take for granted. One of those things is the freedom we have in our country. We are free to go to camp in the summer and learn about Christ. We are free to move about without getting permission from our government first. We are free in many other ways. A suggestion: when you pray, give thanks to God for the freedoms you have - and name them specifically.

OCTOBER 25 DEUTERONOMY 17:1-7

Life was pretty rugged in those old times. Worshipping a

god other than the Lord received the death sentence. If that penalty were in force today, there would be a lot of dead people around. People today worship false gods such as those in eastern religions, or the "gods" of money, success, and getting new things.

Even though the death sentence for such false worship is not in force today, that kind of sin is still serious. It is the Lord who has made us. It is the Lord who keeps us alive by the bodily functions He has created in us. It is the Lord who sent His Son to die for us to bring us eternal life. Only the Lord, then, deserves our thanks and worship.

OCTOBER 26   DEUTERONOMY 17:14-20

God's laws are for everyone. Even the king. It would be very easy for a ruler to think he was above keeping the laws. He was the people's leader. They obeyed his laws. Why should he submit to anyone else's laws?

The best leaders, however, first learn to obey. The Lord Jesus is the King of kings and Lord of lords. Yet He obeyed His Father, even to the point of death on the cross for you and me (Philippians 2:8). If you wish to be a leader among boys or girls, and later among men and women, you must first learn to follow. For the Christian that means, above all, keeping God's laws.

OCTOBER 27   DEUTERONOMY 18:1-8

The priests of Israel had the special job of serving the Lord in His temple. Because of that job, they could not work in the fields to grow their food. So God arranged that the other Israelites gave some of their food to feed the priests and their families.

With their special position also went some restrictions. The priests could not own a part of the Promised Land (verses 1,2). Being a Christian is also special. But it means we are under restrictions, too. We must live not as we please, but as He pleases. In the end we shall see that way as best.

OCTOBER 28   DEUTERONOMY 18:9-14

Some of the laws recorded in Deuteronomy do not apply to our time. For example, those in chapter 14:1-21. God has changed His ways of dealing with us. Other laws are as up-to-date as tomorrow. Such laws are these that apply to witchcraft (verses 10, 11). At present a renewed interest has arisen in witches, wizards, and all that is usually called occult. The Christian's guide to life is not to be any of these. Instead he is to look to the Bible that God has given to us, and be taught by His Spirit.

OCTOBER 29   DEUTERONOMY 18:15-22

The events recorded in Deuteronomy took place centuries before the Lord Jesus came to earth. Yet these verses contain a promise of Christ's coming into the world (verses 15, 18). Much later the Apostle Peter refers to the fulfilment of the promise (Acts 3:18-22). Note that the prophet like Moses would not speak merely his own ideas. He would say what God had commanded him to say (verse 18). Jesus said about Himself, "The Son can do nothing by Himself. He does only what He sees the Father doing. What the Father does, the Son does" (John 5:19). "I and my Father are one" (John 10:30).

OCTOBER 30   DEUTERONOMY 19:1-7

Someone had been killed. The duty of the closest relative of the dead person was to take revenge on the killer. Sometimes the killing was accidental (verse 5). That did not matter. The relative had to do his duty. God here provides for six places in which the accidental killer could be safe (verses 7, 9).

The Bible warns us to flee from Hell. We may not like it, but Hell is real (Matthew 13:49,50). Now, just as God provided safe places for the accidental killer, he has provided a way of escape from Hell. That way of escape is ours if we accept Jesus Christ as our personal Saviour (Acts 16:31).

OCTOBER 31

DEUTERONOMY 22:1-8

If your dad or mom works in a factory, you may have overheard them talk about accidents and safety. People are careless of the rights of others and of their well-being. So rules have to be made in order that others will not get hurt.

In these verses some rules are set down so that the Israelites would be careful about other people's possessions (verses 1-4) and safety (verse 8). That is part of what it means to love your neighbour as yourself (Leviticus 19:18; Mark 12:31).

NOVEMBER 1   DEUTERONOMY 26:1-10

We have been taught, since we were tiny, to say "thank you" when we are given something. Has saying "thank you" become such a habit that you sometimes forget to say it?

The Israelites forgot again and again to thank God for His goodness to them. God had to constantly remind them of their rescue from Egypt and of His leading to the Promised Land. In chapter 26, God makes a law that His people must bring the best of their crops to Him as a way of saying "thank you" when they reach the Promised Land. God even tells them what to say.

Must God *order* us to thank Him for His love in our

lives? Or do we thank Him every day because we love Him? For a Christian, every day is Thanksgiving Day!

NOVEMBER 2   DEUTERONOMY 28:1-14

What wonderful promises God made to His people! He was going to make them happy in every area of life. He would give them large families, plentiful crops and many animals. Their enemies would fall before them. Everyone would know that they were God's people. BUT, they had to obey ALL of God's commandments.

Today God promises Christians many wonderful things. God's people can share everything that Jesus had from His Father. However, we cannot share God's gifts unless we are part of God's family. Jesus died on the cross to pay for our sins, but we must ask Him to forgive us. Just as the Israelites had to obey God, we must turn from our old ways to obey Him. Then we will have the most wonderful promise from God... the promise of living forever with Him.

NOVEMBER 3   DEUTERONOMY 28:15-26

Have you ever lived through a day where just everything you did was wrong? Perhaps you are a little like the disobedient Israelites.

Yesterday we read that if God's people obeyed Him, their life would be happy. Today God warns His people of what will happen if they disobey Him. Instead of all the good things that could happen, the most horrible things will come as punishment. The choice was up to the Israelites.

Today, the choice is up to you. If you, as a Christian, choose to obey God, He will give you all good things to enjoy. Read 1 Timothy 6:17. If you choose to disobey Him, your Heavenly Father may have to "spank" you to correct you. Look up Hebrews 12:5,6.

"Choose you this day whom ye will serve."

NOVEMBER 4   DEUTERONOMY 29:1-9

How could the Israelites be so blind to all the things God had done for them? God worked miracles to rescue them from

Egypt. They wore the same shoes and clothes for 40 years and *nothing* wore out! God fed them with manna - His special food. All their enemies were defeated. But the people still had to be *told* to thank and obey the Lord.

Of course, we aren't so stupid. God provides us with food and clothes. He's given us parents who love and guide us in our lives. He's given us teachers that we might learn to live in His world. Because He loves us, He's given us His Son to save us from being punished for our sins, and we thank Him every day for all His gifts.

Don't we?

NOVEMBER 5   DEUTERONOMY 29:10-21

Moses knew the Israelites well. He knew that even though all the people "looked" as though they were ready to be God's people, some of them wanted to worship other gods in their hearts. What did Moses say would happen to these people? Read verse 20.

Have you ever "played the part" of being a Christian, just to get your parents or friends off your back? Do you think you can "get by" just acting like a Christian, without really accepting God at all? In the book of Revelation, God warned a whole church that only "played the part." Read Revelation 3:14-19.

Before God, there are no phoney Christians!

NOVEMBER 6   DEUTERONOMY 29:22-29

Today we continue to read of God's punishment for those Israelites who disobey Him. All the horrible curses mentioned in chapter 28 will come upon them. Other nations will see what God has done to them. They will be thrown out of their own land into a strange land.

These prophecies have come true! Twice, the entire nation of Israel was taken captive by other nations. After Jesus died, the city of Jerusalem was ruined and the Jews were scattered all over the world. They have only started returning to their homeland in the last few years. For hundreds of years, Palestine has been dry and barren.

Wouldn't their lives have been happier if they had learned to obey God's law? Do you obey God?

NOVEMBER 7   DEUTERONOMY 30:1-10

These ten verses are a beautiful picture of the forgiveness of God. Verse 1 shows that Israel would pay for her sins through the curses God described. Then when she turned to God again, He would welcome her with open arms, forgive, and bless her.

Our sins also have to be paid for, because God cannot stand sin. But when Jesus died on the cross, He paid for our sin with His own life. Because He was God's Son, He rose from the dead so that we could live forever with Him.

However, just like Israel, we must confess our sin to God, turn from sin and obey Him with *all* our heart. Then He promises to accept us.

If we confess our sins, He is faithful and just to forgive us our sins, and to cleanse us from all unrighteousness."

NOVEMBER 8   DEUTERONOMY 31:1-6

For about 60 years, Moses had led the children of Israel towards the Promised Land. He had taught and reminded them of God's laws. Now he begins his farewell speech.

Do you remember why Moses couldn't enter the Promised Land, after all that work? Read Numbers 20:7-12. Even Moses disobeyed God and had to be punished. But Moses didn't pout or complain. Instead, he encouraged his people and reminded them that God was always with them.

How do we act when we are punished? Do we have temper tantrums in front of parents or friends? Do we sit in a corner with a long face? Or do we accept what we deserve, ask for forgiveness, and go on living as a better person for God?

NOVEMBER 9   DEUTERONOMY 31:7-13

The time has come for Moses to appoint a new leader over Israel. God had already named him in Deuteronomy 1:38. Do you remember who it was? He had been a mighty warrior, the servant of Moses, and one of the spies sent into Canaan. His faith in God was strong, even when others doubted. Does he sound qualified for the job? Verse 8 tells us that Joshua would succeed because God would guide him.

Verses 9 to 13 show us the importance of reading God's Word. Do verses 10 and 11 mean that God's Word should be read only every seven years? No! This was a special public reading at one of the Jewish feasts. If we are "to hear and learn to fear God," then we must read His Word every day.

NOVEMBER 10   DEUTERONOMY 31:14-21

What happens to you when everything goes right? Do you forget about God? Why should you read and pray when life's going great?

God knew that as soon as the Israelites "had it easy" in Canaan, they would forget Him. How sad that made God. The Bible says that God would hide His face from them because of their sin.

Think over this question: Isn't forgetting about God a sin that will lead you to other sins? Don't have a case of Bad Memory like the children of Israel. Remember the words of Psalm 143:8:

"Cause me to hear Thy lovingkindness in the morning; for in Thee do I trust: cause me to know the way wherein I should walk; for I lift up my soul unto Thee."

NOVEMBER 11   DEUTERONOMY 31:22-30

Moses gave his whole life to God to rescue the children of Israel. Now he would sing them his last song. The song wasn't thanking the people, or telling them how good they'd been. It was a song about their sin. Moses must have been very sad.

Like Moses, our parents give us the best years of their lives, and almost everything they have. They do so much for us, yet we still slap them in the face with our back talk and our disobedience. It must make them sad.

God gave up His Son for us. He is constantly trying to make us like Jesus, but we give Him the worst treatment of all. We ignore Him, we disobey Him, we try to run away from Him. How very sad God must be.

What kind of a song would your life write?

NOVEMBER 12   DEUTERONOMY 32:1-17

The saddest part of Moses' song is found in verses 15 to 17. God had rescued, led, loved and provided for the children of Israel for 60 years. Now He knew that as soon as they reached the riches of the Promised Land, they would forget Him and worship false gods.

Of course in this country, we don't worship idols, so we could never be guilty like the Israelites. What about that TV program you "worship" Sunday night instead of going to church? What about those cool kids at school - you'd never let them know you are a Christian! What about your "worship" of books you shouldn't read? How about the "worship time" you spend in front of that mirror?

ME - guilty like the Israelites?

NOVEMBER 13   DEUTERONOMY 33:1-12

When a father was dying in Moses' day, he gave his sons a "blessing." It was something like a will - a promise of what the sons would inherit. In today's reading, Moses begins his blessing to each of the 12 tribes of Israel. These blessings were really given by God through Moses.

I think Benjamin's tribe received the most beautiful blessing. This tribe was called "beloved of the Lord." They were promised safety, and the constant "covering protection" of God. They were also promised that God's temple would be built on Benjamin's land in the Promised Land.

If we are Christians, Jesus has given us a wonderful blessing. Read John 14:1-3. What is God's promise to us?

NOVEMBER 14   DEUTERONOMY 33:13-21

Have you noticed how each tribe is promised a particular place and job? Reuben was to be a "pioneer" tribe, and Moses prayed for their protection. Levi's tribe were to be priests. Joseph's tribe inherited rich land and would be wealthy farmers. Zebulun was given land near the sea, so the people became seamen and traders. Issachar's tribe were quiet people, working at home.

Those jobs weren't all exciting, but they were all necessary. Have you ever felt that you can't do anything for God? The Bible says that, just as we need *every* part of our body, God needs *every* Christian doing his own little job to finish His work.

God has put you right where you are, just as He placed the 12 tribes of Israel. Be happy in God's place.

NOVEMBER 15   DEUTERONOMY 34:1-12

What happened to Moses? God took him to the top of a very high mountain and showed him the land he'd spent 60 years trying to reach. Then, even though he was healthy (he didn't even need glasses!), Moses died, and GOD buried him. Isn't that exciting?

We don't like to talk about dying, but for a Christian, death is beautiful. God sees that our work on earth is done. He has finished working IN us, so He takes us to be with Him. That's what happened to Moses.

Verses 10-12 were put in the Bible to honour Moses. What is the most beautiful thing said about Moses' life? *The Lord knew Moses face to face.* Could someone say that about you?

NOVEMBER 16   PSALM 50:1-23

Today, the poet Asaph writes the same truths about disobedient people that Moses wrote many years before. God's Word never changes.

God is the ONLY One who can, and will judge our Christian lives. In verses 7 to 15 we see that those Israelites who thought only about *what* and *how often* they sacrificed to God, didn't please God. God wanted them to thank and praise

Him. Do you think more about how often you go to church, or about the God you go to worship?

Read verses 16 to 22 again. Do you speak well of God, but get angry when you are corrected? Do you say you obey

God, but let others cheat with you in school? Do you say you love Jesus and hate that kid in your class? God is pleased only with people whose lives are ordered by Him.

NOVEMBER 17   PSALM 51:1-19

What does the word "confess" really mean? David had a man murdered so that he could steal the man's wife. God told him about his sin, and David had to confess. Psalm 51 is his prayer.

David asks God to forgive his sin, because David cannot forget about it. Other people always get hurt when we sin, but David knew his sin hurt God more than anyone. He had disobeyed God.

David asks God for a clean heart, and a spirit that will not turn away from God. He asks that God's Holy Spirit would stay with him, and that he would again be happy in God's salvation.

Since David has learned his lesson, he will be able to help others who sin. And finally, David praises God for His forgiveness.

NOVEMBER 18   PSALM 53:1-6

If you have ever thought of yourself as a "good person," read Psalm 53 and you'll probably change your mind.

Without God, there isn't one person who is good. Everything we do is worthless. We do things for ourselves and not for God. We think we can run our own lives, so who needs God?

David knew people needed God to save them, and he cried out for a Saviour. Today we have that Saviour. Jesus Christ is the only One who can make our lives worth something for God. Jesus died for you. Have you asked Him to wash away your sin? Does He control your life?

NOVEMBER 19   PSALM 55:1-23

"As soon as people find out I'm a Christian, they scorn me out!"..."Sometimes I'm scared stiff to even go to school." "I wish I could fly off somewhere so people would leave me alone!"

Have you ever felt this way? David did. But compared to David, you have it easy. His enemies wanted to kick him off his throne - maybe even kill him! One of the enemy leaders used to be his good friend.

David found the answer to his problems in God. Prayer was one of the most important things in his life. David prayed at least three times a day. Do you manage three minutes?

Take David's suggestion in verse 22 to solve your problems: *"Cast your problems upon the Lord, and He will continually give you strength."*

NOVEMBER 20   PSALM 56:1-13

David was a very brave man, but his bravery came from his trust in God. He admitted there were times when he was really afraid, but he trusted God. When in trouble, did David beg God to get him out? No! Four times David praised God for His faithfulness. Because he trusted God, it didn't matter what men did to him.

How do you react when God puts you in a rough spot? Do you sit down, cry, and ask God why? Are you tempted to "chuck this whole Christianity bit"? Remember Psalm 56:11. It is much more important to trust God, than to fear men.

NOVEMBER 21   PSALM 62:1-12

Once again David tells of his trust in God, no matter what men do to him. But he also tells us to trust God at ALL times.

We have seen that David was a praying man. In verse 8, David commands us to be the same. What does it mean to "pour out your heart before" God? Have you ever taken the time to tell God absolutely *everything* on your mind: all your problems; all that makes you happy; what you are afraid of; all of your questions about Him; that you love Him? God is your Saviour, and as verse 8 says, He is your shelter. Pour out everything to Him, your Shelter, and you will come to know Him as your dearest Friend.

NOVEMBER 22   PSALM 65:1-13

Everywhere we look on this earth, we see the results of God's power. Verses 6-13 describe many of God's works.

Remember that clear night at camp, when you stood staring at the billions of stars splashed across that inky sky?

Somehow you *knew* God had put them there, and you could praise Him. But did you praise Him for the third day of rain? Verses 9 and 10 tell us that God gave us that rain. Remember that afternoon when the storm came across the lake, churning and flashing at everything in its path? When the storm had gone, the lake was like glass. Verse 7 tells us that God stills the waves. In fact, He created and controls *all* of nature.

And this great God chooses us, Christians, to be His people. Praise Him!

NOVEMBER 23   PSALM 69:1-21

David had a rough time in life, didn't he? In these Psalms, it seems as though his enemies were always chasing him. But what did all those hard times make David do? He constantly called on God. Trouble kept David praising God.

Perhaps it shouldn't always take trouble to keep us talking to God, but sometimes it does. We should trust Him just as much when life is running smoothly, but we don't. Can't we remember that God loves us, and longs to talk with us every day?

"Look unto Jesus at ALL times,
All that you need is in Him;
Whether you walk in the sunlight,
Or when the way grows dim."
— *Ida Guirey*

NOVEMBER 24   PSALM 69:22-36

Have you been wondering about David's thoughts towards his enemies? They are certainly hard thoughts. David even asks God to punish them for their sin.

David was a man who knew how God hated sin. God couldn't stand to look at sin. These enemies of David seemed to be men who again and again turned from God and disobeyed Him. David hated the SIN in these men, and wanted to see it destroyed. He did not hate the men.

How should we react to those who sin? We, as David, must hate their sin, and not be afraid to tell them how they are hurting God. But we must also tell them of Jesus' salvation and pray for them with God's love in our hearts.

NOVEMBER 25   TITUS 1:1-9

Today we begin Paul's letter to Titus, telling Titus how to help the Christian church in Crete.

Paul lists the qualities a man should have before being allowed to work in the church. Let's look at one of these qualities.

His children were to be well-behaved and faithful. Many of you have fathers who work in the church. The Bible says they have a responsibility to raise you as obedient children, and they try very hard to do just that. *But what about you?* The Bible commands, "Children, obey your parents in the Lord." It also says, "Honour your father and your mother..." Neither command adds the words, "...when you think they're right!" You have a responsibility to be well-behaved and obedient children.

NOVEMBER 26   TITUS 1:10-16

It seems that the Cretian Church had trouble with out-siders telling them how to live their Christian lives. The trouble was, these people didn't teach from the Bible. They taught things that sounded good to them, or said things they were bribed to say.

Does that remind you of school? Many of the things which you are taught don't go along with the Bible's teaching. In verse 9 Paul said that bishops had to know Scripture to be able to show these liars how wrong they were. So must we know God's Word, and know WHY we believe it is true. God may then use you to teach your teachers the truth about Himself.

NOVEMBER 27   TITUS 2:1-8

I once knew a girl at camp who never seemed to do a thing wrong! We went to camp together for about three years. I never saw her get angry, and she never said an unkind word about anyone. She was generous, always on time, and never lazy. She was quietly more like Jesus than anyone else I've ever known.

Paul commanded Titus to be just like that girl. He was to *regularly* be an example of good works. In fact, he was to be so much like Jesus, that nobody could say one bad thing about him!

And God wants you to be just the same! How? Philippians 4:13 says: "I can do *all* things through *Christ*, who strengtheneth me."

NOVEMBER 28   TITUS 2:9-15

Do you *really* want Jesus to return to earth? I used to pray that He'd wait just long enough so that I could get married. Isn't that selfish? But it's very hard for us as young people to wish Jesus would come back!

Titus probably wasn't very old, but Paul told him not to think much about things here on earth. He was to make his life count for Jesus, so he could hardly wait for Christ's return.

Can we make ourselves feel that way? The more you are with the person you love, the more you love that person. The more time you spend with the Lord, the more you love Him and long to look at His face. Read your Bible, pray, and watch for Jesus' return.

NOVEMBER 29   TITUS 3:1-8

It surely is easy to get into an argument - even a fight! And it's always the *other* person's fault, right?

But Paul says we aren't to say anything bad about other people. NOTHING! Nor are we to fight. After all, we used to be just like those people. We were disobedient, we lied, we did whatever we pleased, we hated and we were jealous.

But then - for no reason in us, Jesus gave His life to save us. Just because He loved us, God gave us everlasting life. He gave us His Holy Spirit to guide us. Knowing this, and knowing Him should change every action of our lives. Our lives are now Christ's - our actions are controlled by Him. Or, they should be.

NOVEMBER 30   TITUS 3:9-15

How many times have you argued with someone about the Bible? And how often have you argued with non-Christians about something in the Bible? Paul says these arguments are useless, and are only to "show off our smarts."

"Then how can I convince people that the Bible is true?" You can't! That job belongs to the Holy Spirit. It's your job to tell them *what* the Bible says. God's Spirit does the work of making them believe it.

"Is that all I can do?" No. 1 Timothy 2:1-4 says: *"I exhort... that...prayers...be made for all men...for this is good and acceptable in the sight of God, our Saviour; Who will have all men to be saved, and to come unto the knowledge of the truth."*

DECEMBER 1   PHILEMON 1:1-9

Did you ever really need someone to plead your case for you? Paul did that for Onesimus in this letter to Philemon. Paul knew his friend Philemon quite well and knew he could depend on him. He did not hesitate to ask him for a favour.

Make a list of Philemon's good qualities. He was a great guy. Now check the list and see if a friend could say the same things about you.

DECEMBER 2   PHILEMON 1:10-25

Onesimus ran away! Perhaps he was tired of being a slave and always having someone tell him what to do. For whatever reason, he left his master Philemon and somehow got to Rome. Great! He is in the big city enjoying himself. Wrong! He is in jail. Poor Onesimus! Well, not exactly poor. He met Paul there and, through that contact, came to Christ. Paul sent him back to Philemon that he may fulfil his duty. Do you sometimes feel like Onesimus - want to run away from your home or your job? Paul's advice to Onesimus was to go back home to Philemon. When God saves us, He expects us to show this in love to our family and by doing our work well, whatever it is.

DECEMBER 3   ZECHARIAH 1:12-17

God chose the people of Israel to be His special people and gave them laws to guide them through life. They did not keep these laws, so He had to punish them. He permitted the Assyrians to fight them and take them prisoners to Babylon. After 70 years there, some of them were allowed to come home to Jerusalem.

Zechariah was God's messenger or prophet to this group of people. God told Zechariah that He was very unhappy with the nations around Israel. They had treated His people in a very cruel way. However, God was going to build His nation Israel and their cities again. Jerusalem would once more be very prosperous.

DECEMBER 4   ZECHARIAH 2:1-5

God promised to rebuild Jerusalem. The angel measured the city to see if it would be big enough to hold all the people. In verse 5 the Lord promised He would be like a wall of fire to protect them and He would be the glory of the city.

We also need God to protect us. We are not likely to see a circle of fire around us, but He has promised that His angels will guard those who trust Him. Sometimes we need His protection against wicked people. Other times against temptations in our hearts or from Satan. Depend on God, whatever it is. Then thank Him. He will be honoured when we do this. He will be the glory of the city in verse 5; so He will be honoured in our lives when we depend on Him.

DECEMBER 5   ZECHARIAH 2:10-13

The vision given to Zechariah showed him that God will one day live on earth among His people. At that time many other nations will gather to Jerusalem. Since that promise, Israel has looked forward to this with joy. God has a promise for us today (John 14:23).When we trust in Jesus Christ, He promises to live in our hearts. There is nothing that gives more joy than this.

DECEMBER 6   ZECHARIAH 3:1-10

Sometimes the Bible draws word pictures to help us understand some important truth. Here we see Joshua. His clothes are filthy (much dirtier than when you have been on a canoe trip). The Lord said to the angel, "Take those dirty things off him." Then He said to Joshua, "I have taken away your guilt." That, my friend, is what Christ can do for you... take away all your sin and guilt. Then the Lord said, "I will give you some fine, clean clothes." That is another picture of what Christ can do for us. When we trust Him, He will put His righteousness - or rightness - on us. He makes us all right to stand in front of Him - something we could never do if our sins were not taken away.

DECEMBER 7   ZECHARIAH 4:1-6

The angel talked with Zechariah again. This message was for Zerubbabel. He was the man who was to build the Lord's temple in Jerusalem again. He would work with the few Jews who had returned there from Babylon - that place where they had been captive for 70 years. They were weak, they were afraid and there were very few of them.

Maybe there is some job God has for you to do. You say, "Oh, but Lord, I'm too young; I don't know anything about that; I have no one to help me." What did God say to Zerubbabel? "Not by might, nor by power, will you do this building, but by My Spirit." Christ has the same word for us today and we "can do all things through Christ who strengthens" us (Philippians 4:13).

DECEMBER 8   ZECHARIAH 4:7-10

Zerubbabel began the building, of course, at the foundation. What a lot of back-breaking work... no bulldozers! What could anybody see after all this effort? You don't see much of the foundation of any building when it is finished, but it is most important. Verse 10 tells us not to despise a small beginning. Your first efforts of service for the Lord may go unnoticed by your friends but God will know all about it. Nothing escapes His attention or is too small for His reward.

DECEMBER 9   ZECHARIAH 6:9-15

This is the second time in Zechariah that we read of "The Branch." In chapter 3:8 God promised to send His servant "The Branch." That helps us to realize that "The Branch" is another name given to Christ. Joshua represents Christ when he is given a crown (verse 11). Christ will wear a crown one day and He will rule as king over the whole earth. Zerubbabel rebuilt the temple in Jerusalem. We learn here of yet another temple that Christ will build when He comes back to earth. People from many lands will help build that temple of the Lord (verse 15).

DECEMBER 10   ZECHARIAH 9:9-10

Do the words of verse 9 sound familiar? You may be thinking of Matthew 21:1-5. Read this now and see how Zechariah's words came true when Christ rode into Jerusalem.

Look at Zechariah 11:10-13. Where have you read about thirty pieces of silver? Matthew 27:1-10. Christ received a great welcome from the people but soon Judas betrayed Him for a few dollars. We are horrified at Judas' action. But think carefully. Perhaps one day you said, "I'd like Jesus to be my Saviour." Since then have you ever traded Him for something - like being "in" with the crowd or cheating to make a good mark? Tell Him about it and ask Him to be Lord of your life again.

DECEMBER 11   ZECHARIAH 13:1-9

Do you sing in Sunday School, "There's a fountain flowing deep and wide"? You may know then that the fountain comes from Christ and will wash away all our sins. Have you ever held your face under the water tap when you were hot and dusty? It is a great feeling, but you may not get your face very clean. When we come to Christ, He takes away all our sin. We have God's Word for it in verse 1.

Look back to chapter 12:10, "They shall look upon me whom they have pierced." John 19:37 tells us when this happened to Christ. Now read verse 7 in chapter 13. Christ said these words to His disciples in Matthew 26:31. Zechariah wrote about many things that plainly happened to Christ 500 years later.

DECEMBER 12   ACTS 1:1-14

Luke wrote this book of Acts. He is the same person who wrote the story of the Lord Jesus in Luke's Gospel. Now he writes about what happened after the Lord Jesus rose from the dead. Peter, John and James were going to have some exciting days. But first of all Jesus told them they would receive the Holy Spirit. With His Spirit, they would have great power. This was true power and nothing phoney like some TV magic.

In verse 4 the Holy Spirit is promised. What other promise was given to the Christians? Read verse 11. Do you suppose these two great promises (1) the Holy Spirit, (2) Christ will return, had any effect on the Christians? What did they do when they returned to the city? Read verse 14.

DECEMBER 13   ACTS 1:15-26

Jesus had given Judas the opportunity to be His close friend and to tell people about Him (Mark 3:13-19). Judas failed miserably. He wasted his opportunity. Now Matthias is chosen to take his place. He would be one of the 12 apostles. What a privilege! Jesus gives you the opportunity to become one of His children through trusting Him. Then you too can tell others about Him. You have many other opportunities such as reading the Bible and going to Sunday School where a teacher helps you understand God's Word. And what a great opportunity you had last summer - going to camp! God wants you to make the best use of these opportunities.

DECEMBER 14   ACTS 2:1-13

Christ promised the disciples that His Spirit would come to live in them (Acts 1:8). Now this happened suddenly, with the sound like the roar of a strong wind. When you trust

Jesus as your Saviour, His Spirit will come to you too, but not with the sound of a rushing wind. The moment you believe in Christ, His Holy Spirit comes to stay in your heart. These early Christians talked about the great things God did (verse 11). Did you trust Jesus at camp? Have you told anyone at home about that? God's salvation is His most wonderful work (see Ephesians 2:5). As sinners, we are dead to God but He can make us alive in Christ. Can you think of anything more wonderful than that? Ask the Lord to help you tell somebody about that today.

DECEMBER 15   ACTS 2:14-21

When God promises to do something, you can count on Him doing it. In verses 16-18 Peter reminded the people that many years ago the prophet Joel said that God would send His Spirit. Yesterday we read how this began. In verses 19-20 Peter talked about things that have not yet happened, but you can be sure they will some day. God never breaks a promise. We may be disappointed when a friend doesn't do what he or she promised. Perhaps they had a very good reason for this and we forgive them. But what God has planned will surely come true.

DECEMBER 16   ACTS 2:22-36

Christ's death was not an accident. It was planned by God, and carried out by wicked men. Here was a Man whom the people called Jesus of Nazareth. God showed them He was more than a man by the miracles He did. But there was a greater sign still to come. Christ took our sins and paid for them by His death. But death could not keep Christ because He was God's Holy One and God raised Him to life. Peter says in verse 32, "We saw Jesus. He is alive again; we are all witnesses to this." This is the message of the resurrection that Peter brought to thousands of people in Jerusalem. It is a message to which we all should listen.

DECEMBER 17   ACTS 2:37-47

"What should we do?" These people realized they had been responsible for the death of the Lord Jesus Christ. They asked a wise question and Peter answered, "Repent." They had rejected Christ and now they were to change their mind and receive Him. Have you ever done that? Our sin helped crucify Christ. We are just like those people in Jerusalem and we too must obey this command to repent.

Now notice what these people did. Write down each activity from verses 41-47. There are ten. Now check off the things you do. If you have obeyed God's command, these things should be a part of your life.

DECEMBER 18   ACTS 3:1-11

As you run across the playground or swim across the pool, have you ever thanked God for strong legs and arms? The man in today's story had never done these things, never been to camp and raced a buddy to the dining room. He had never once walked and he had given up all hope of doing so. He made his living by begging and asked Peter and John for money. They had none, but Peter said, "What I do have is Christ and He can make you walk." Peter took his hand and the man stood up and walked. This was the first of many miracles that the Lord did through His disciples; one of the wonderful acts that give this book its name, "Acts of the Apostles."

DECEMBER 19   ACTS 3:12-18

Not for a minute would Peter and John take credit for healing this man. They pointed out that the Name of Jesus had brought strength to the lame man and made him completely well. They spoke to him in Jesus' Name (verse 6). Many times in Acts you read of something being done in Jesus' Name. Paul tells us in Colossians 3:17 to do all things in the Name of the Lord Jesus. Jesus said in John 14:14 to pray in His Name. This should cause us to consider whether or not our actions and our prayers are worthy of that Name.

DECEMBER 20   ACTS 3:19-26

Peter told these people that Moses, Samuel and many other prophets long ago had predicted that Christ would come. Even when they were children they had learned about this from their teachers and parents. There were certain days set aside for reading and listening to these true stories. We will soon remember on our special day, Christmas, that Christ came to our planet. For those people and for us, Christ came to take away our sin. He wants us to repent and trust in Him. He will forgive our sins. That is why He died and rose again to life.

DECEMBER 21   ACTS 4:1-12

"The Name of Jesus Christ." Here is this phrase again. Peter boldly told the rulers that the sick man was healed through the Name of Jesus. For this they were put in jail. Through Christ, this man could walk for the first time in his life. Peter and John told the people about this. They told them that Christ died and rose from the dead that they might live forever. For that they were arrested and put in prison.

Did I hear you say it isn't fair? So what did Peter and John do? They kept on preaching the same message, "salvation through the Name of Jesus Christ," and hoped that the very people who imprisoned them would know their sins forgiven.

DECEMBER 22   ACTS 4:13-22

The rulers recognized Peter and John as friends of Jesus. Peter and John were not doctors or lawyers, nor did they claim to have any healing power apart from Christ. This made the rulers quite nervous. Peter and John were too popular and this would have to stop. They reached a decision: "You are not to talk about Jesus ever again," they said. But Peter and John had a very good reason to question this. Should they obey God or man? Put yourself in Peter and John's place. First, has anyone recognized you as a friend of Christ? Second, if your obedience to God is challenged, do you choose sides with God or man? God promises His blessings to those who obey Him. Read Deuteronomy 7:9.

DECEMBER 23   ACTS 4:23-30

When exciting things happen to us, we love to tell our friends. (Do you remember talking about your great canoe trip?) When Peter and John were set free, they went to their friends to tell them about their experiences. This was a serious business to be told not to talk about Jesus again, but that group of Christians did a wise thing. They asked God to give them courage to continue to preach His Word and do more miracles through the Name of Jesus. I wonder how we would act if we were threatened as they were? Our courage may need to be boosted. There's no better place for that than on our knees before God.

"Dare to be a Daniel,
Dare to stand alone.
Dare to have a purpose
firm,
And dare to make it
known."

Gimme!

DECEMBER 24   ACTS 4:31-37

"That's mine." Does that phrase sound familiar? Do we use it frequently? Little children hold on to their toys and will not let others play with them. Older ones keep their belongings for their own use. We each have things we don't care to share with others. Notice what happened to these Christians when the Holy Spirit filled their hearts. They were of one heart and one soul; and not one claimed his possessions as his own. At Christmastime we are warmed with a glow that causes us to share many things with others. When Christ fills our hearts, our sharing will continue through the year.

DECEMBER 25   ACTS 5:1-11

Yesterday we read about Barnabas selling his land and giving all the money to the church. This generous gift was not because of some law. Barnabas' big heart was filled with love to the Lord and he wanted to give everything to Him. Ananias and Sapphira also sold some property but they thought they could pretend to give all this money and keep a part of it for themselves. We may be guilty of something like that... pretending to be completely devoted to Jesus but keeping Him out of some areas of our life. Ananias and Sapphira died because they thought they could lie to God. This caused the people to ask themselves if they were guilty of any such sin.

DECEMBER 26   ACTS 5:12-16

The wonderful acts of God continued. People from all around Jerusalem came for healing to Peter and John. They tried to get close enough to Peter so that at least his shadow would fall on them. Don't misunderstand this. The Bible does not say Peter's shadow healed them. The healing was by the power of God's Holy Spirit working through Peter.

Notice what people thought of these Christians (verse 13). They spoke well of them and all had the highest regard for them. If we expect people to respect us as Christians, we must let Christ control our lives. Ask Him to fill us with His Spirit and use us in His own way.

DECEMBER 27   ACTS 5:17-28

The High Priest and Sadducees had quite a shock. They put Peter and John in prison but the next morning the doors were still locked and guards on duty, but Peter and John were not there! God had a work for Peter and John to do. That work is described in verse 20: ''Tell the people about this new life." God was not going to let the High Priest nor his friends stop that work. They had crucified the Lord in an attempt to stop His teaching, but He rose from the dead. They locked up the disciples but the angel let them out. Peter and John went on with the work, teaching about Jesus and the new life He gives.

DECEMBER 28   ACTS 5:29-32

"You shall be my witnesses." This is what Jesus said to the disciples before He went back to heaven (Acts 1:8). That is what they were doing - telling the world that Jesus had died to bring forgiveness for sin, that God raised Him back to life. They could be jailed for this (as they now knew) but they would continue to obey God. Many of them were executed for their faithfulness. Some were crucified, others were fed to lions, some were stoned to death, but they obeyed God no matter what the consequences. We may fail to tell others about Christ for fear of lósing popularity or success. Some of the disciples lost their lives for witnessing for Him.

DECEMBER 29   ACTS 5:33-42

The disciples were doing their work thoroughly. Verse 28 tells us they filled Jerusalem with their teaching. No wonder the Pharisees were upset. They could see their traditions being replaced. One councillor, Gamaliel, had some good advice, however. He reminded them of past revolutionaries who had failed. He pointed out that if this is God's work it would prosper and nothing they could do would stop it. This has been true all through history. Read the stories of some missionaries and the great opposition they faced. Yet they carried on their job. When God has a work to do, He will see that it is completed.

DECEMBER 30   ACTS 6:1-7

"Your piece is bigger than mine!" Perhaps we didn't say it aloud but we have thought it? The meat was passed from the far end of the table at camp and you were left with the smallest piece. These people were complaining about that sort of thing. The Christians thought it was important to have everything divided fairly. They chose some special people to do this work. Can you find their four qualifications in verse 3?

DECEMBER 31   ACTS 6:8-15

There are some people who will use any method to try to prove God's Word is untrue. This often happens because the Word bothers our conscience. We recognize something is wrong in our lives. Stephen was preaching God's Word and there were people who didn't like it. How sad it is when we fight against God's teaching! How much better to believe what God tells us in His Word, the Bible!

NOTES

NOTES

NOTES

NOTES

NOTES